Special Edition

Flowers and Drawings of children ready to color.

Watercoloring. Paint photorealistically using beautiful, vivid sketches.

Coloring Like Painting - The Series.
Idea & text & illustrations by: Lech Balcerzak
Raw pics by: pixabay.com

© 2020 by Lech Balcerzak
All rights reserved.
No part of this book may be reproduced or transmitted
without written permission from the author.

Part 1 – Living Drawings (Pencil)

I specialize in photorealistic drawing. I decided to make some children's drawings, because they are the most graceful models, and then they try to paint themselves.

In addition, this part also includes several drawings of women in various poses. This is useful if you want to improve your painting skills.

About New Sketches

My idea: learn to paint by coloring and gradually increasing the difficulty of painting.

So, each sketch is drawn in 2 versions:
1) easy, tonal, even older children can paint on it
2) more difficult, with lines and less detail

My sketches are mostly portraits with no background, so here's a great opportunity to add your own themes. For example, you can draw a road and trees, paint a landscape behind a girl or a beautiful flower next to her, to complete your portrait.

Have a beautiful Christmas,
Lech

PS
To get a beautiful painting (as on the back cover), you need to use soft shading with many layers. You can use pastels, colored pencils with a soft core or watercolors, oil (best effect) or acrylic paints (my favorites, see the Guide). Or everything together (colored pencils + paints).

Don't use markers (unless you want to get kitsch like Andy Warhol), and don't use too much water. This paper doesn't like water.

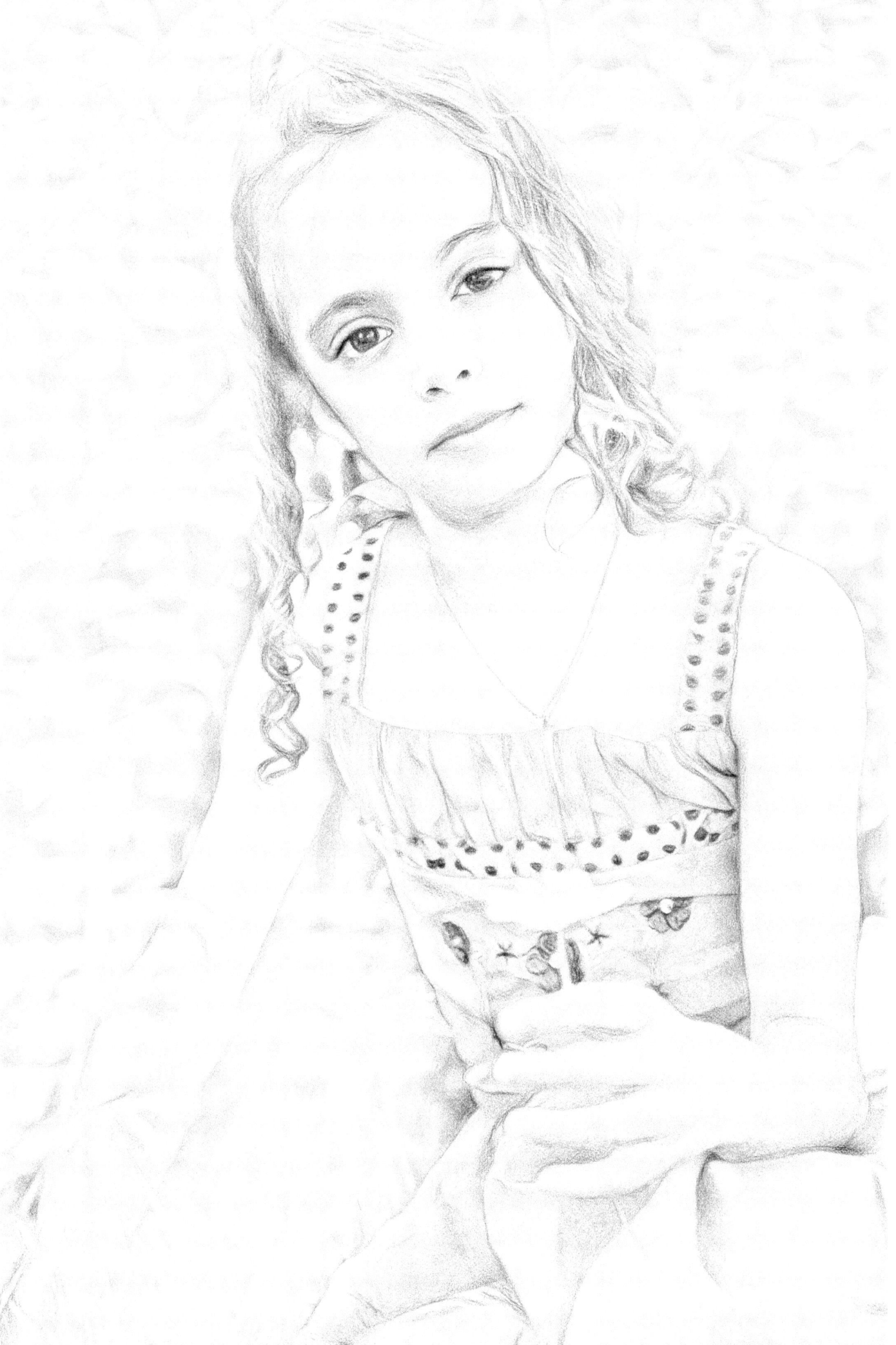

Artwork by/Œuvre par

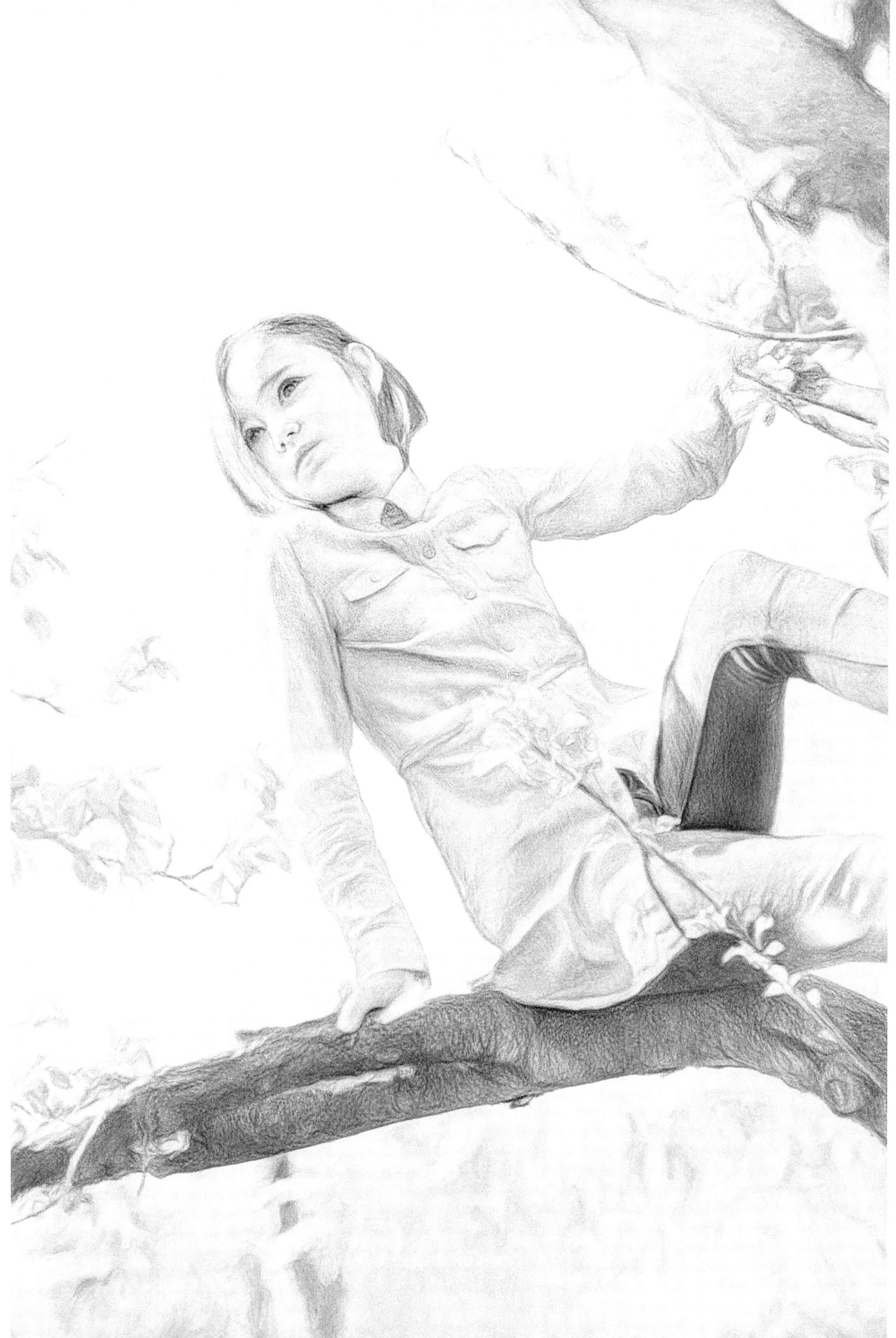

Artounb by l'Œuvre par

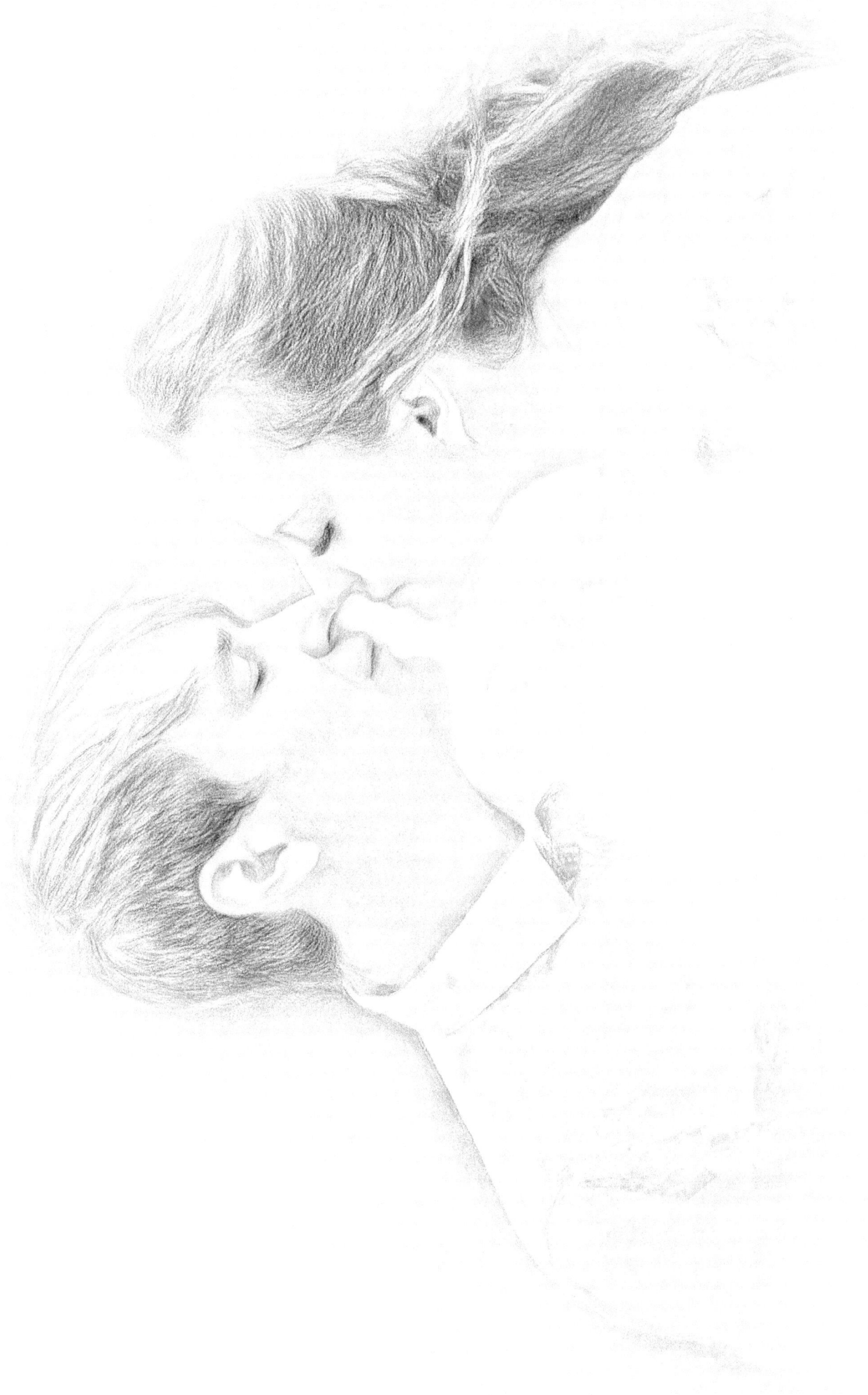

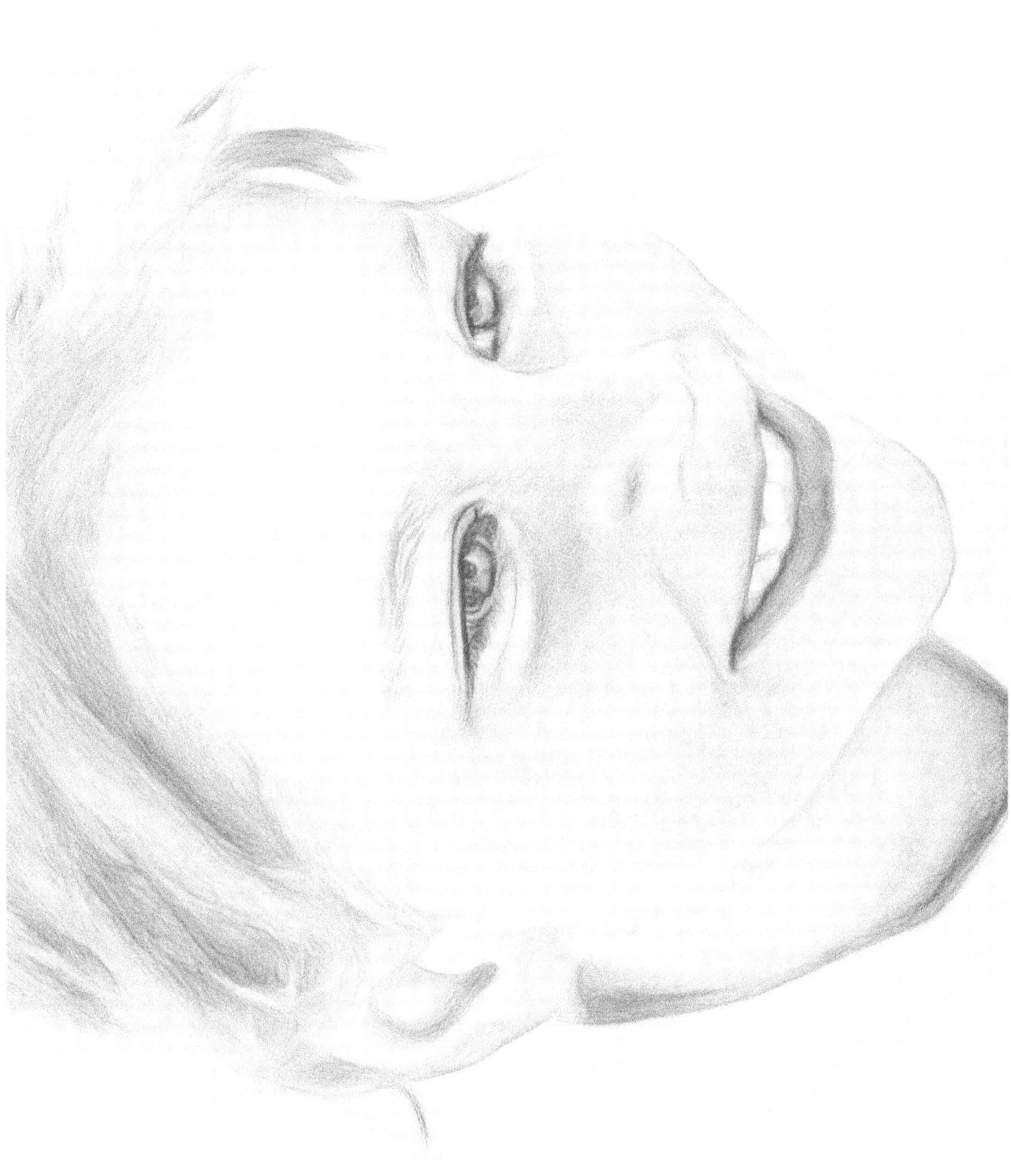

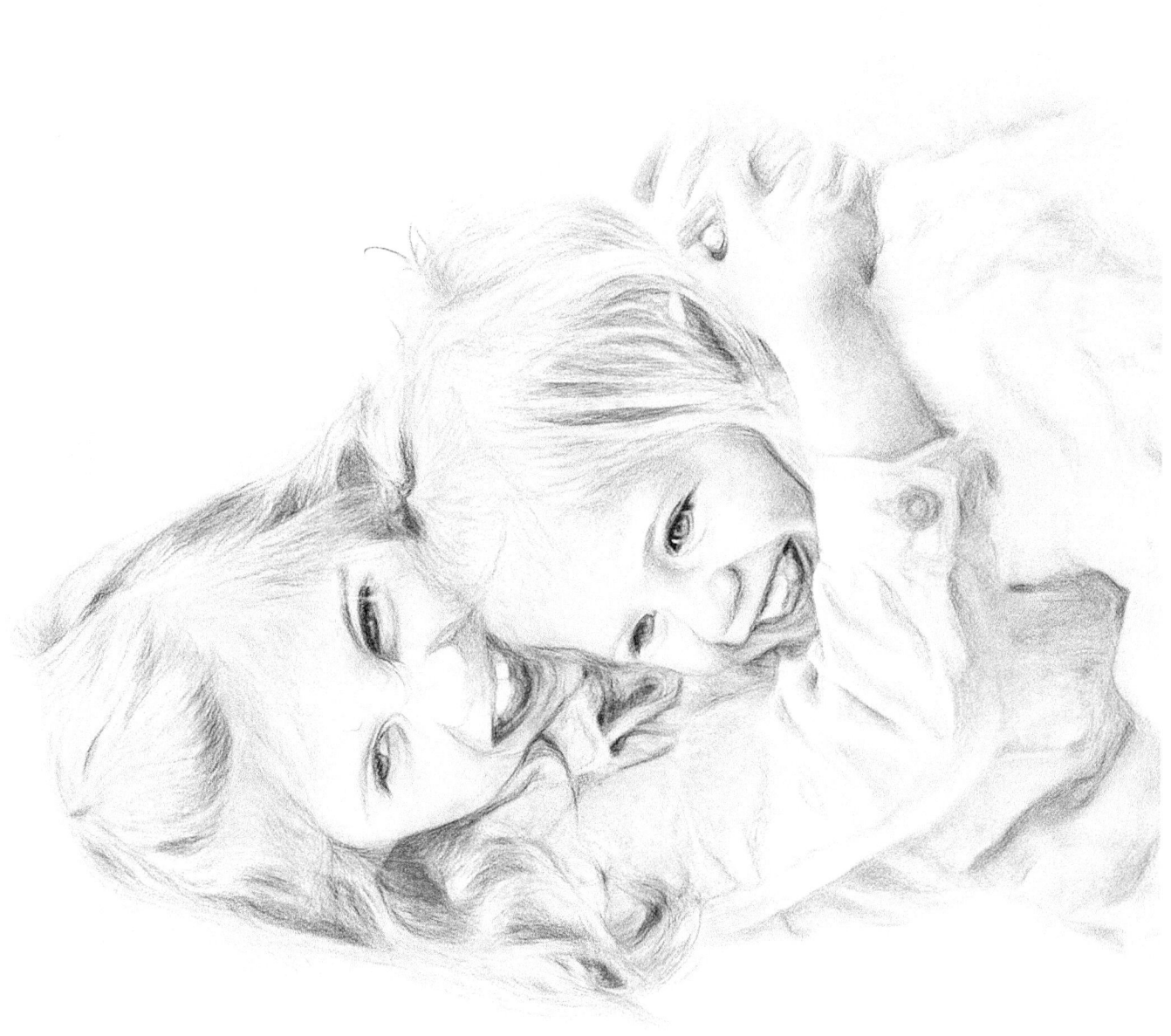

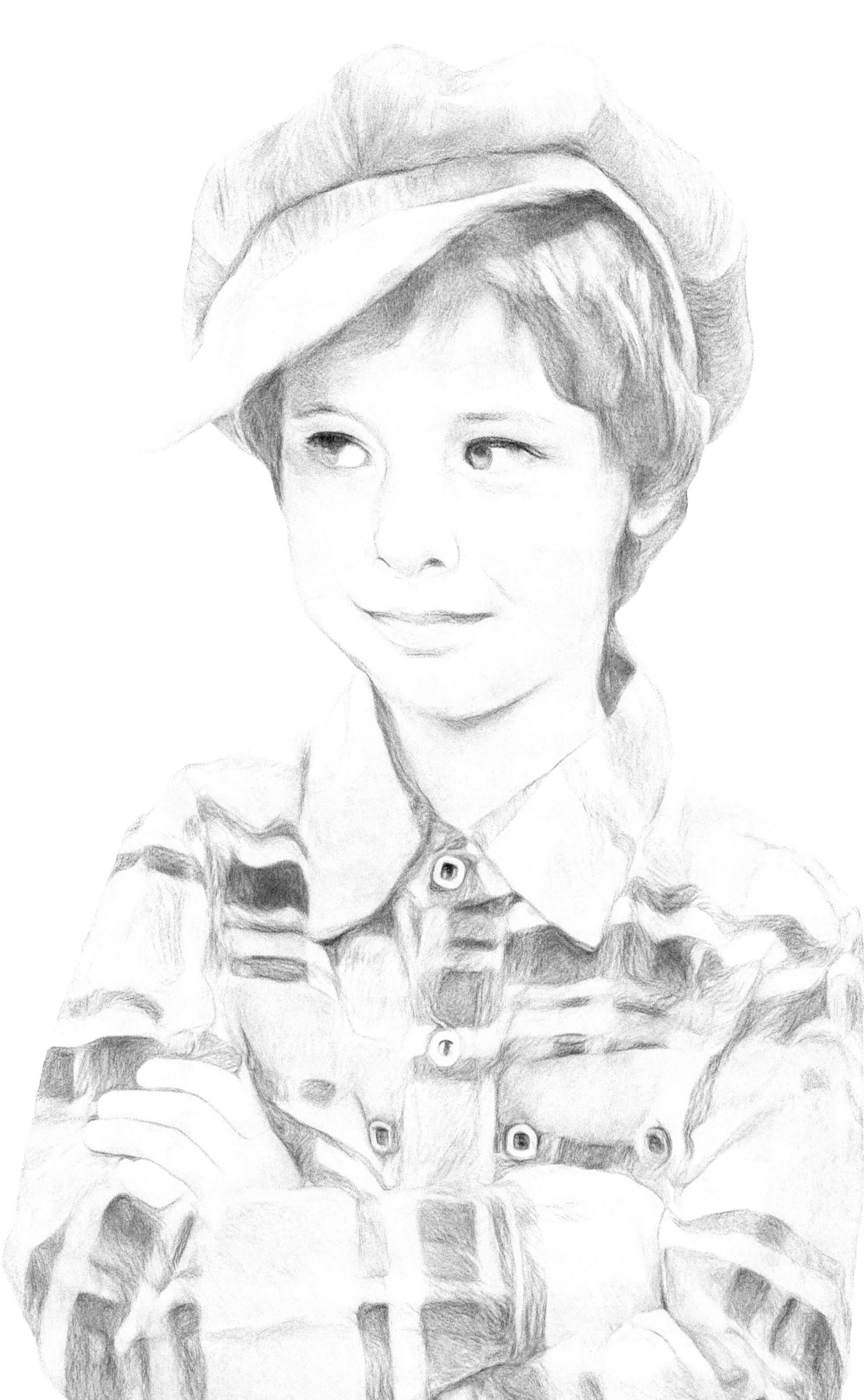

Artwork by J. C.

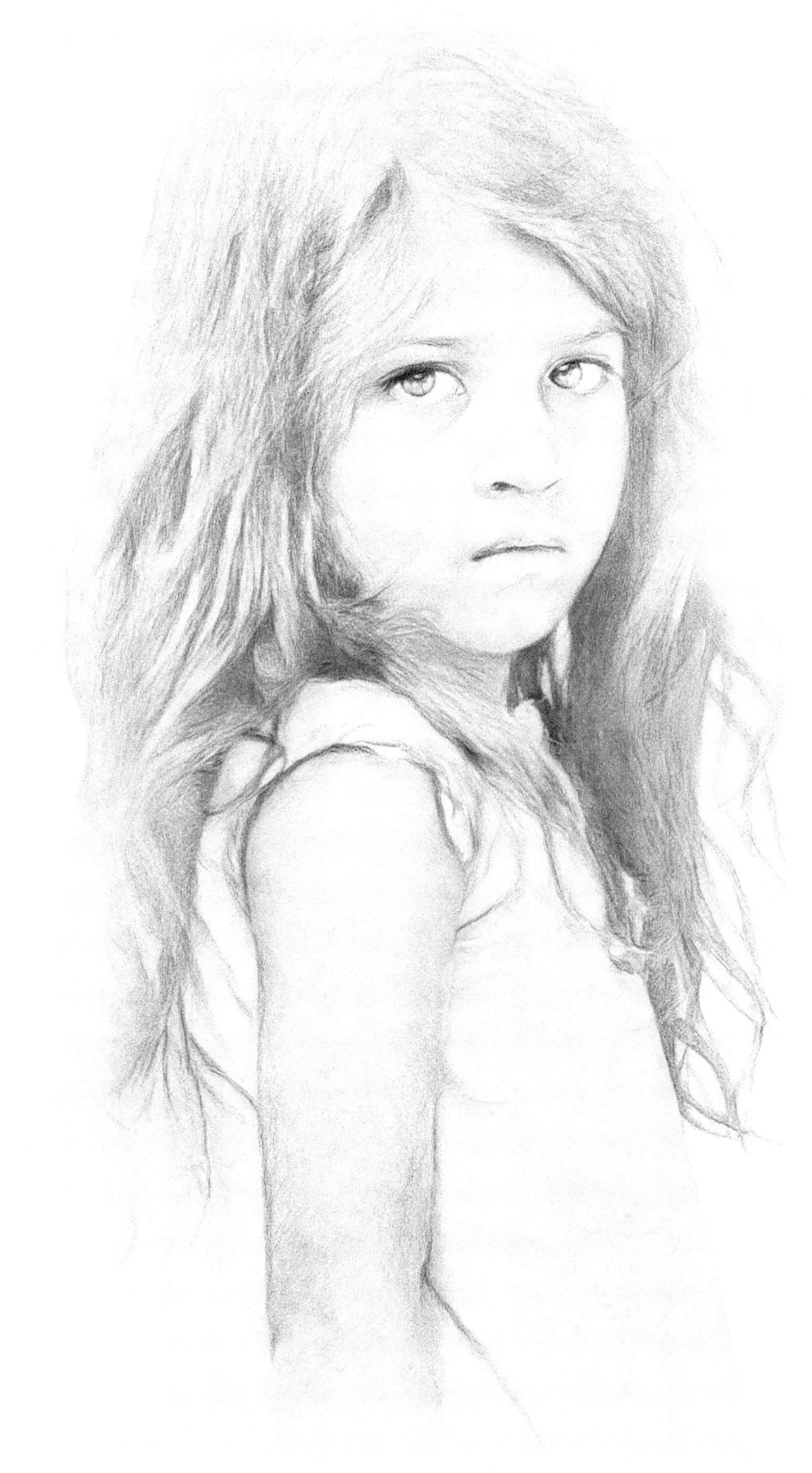

Artwork by / Œuvre par

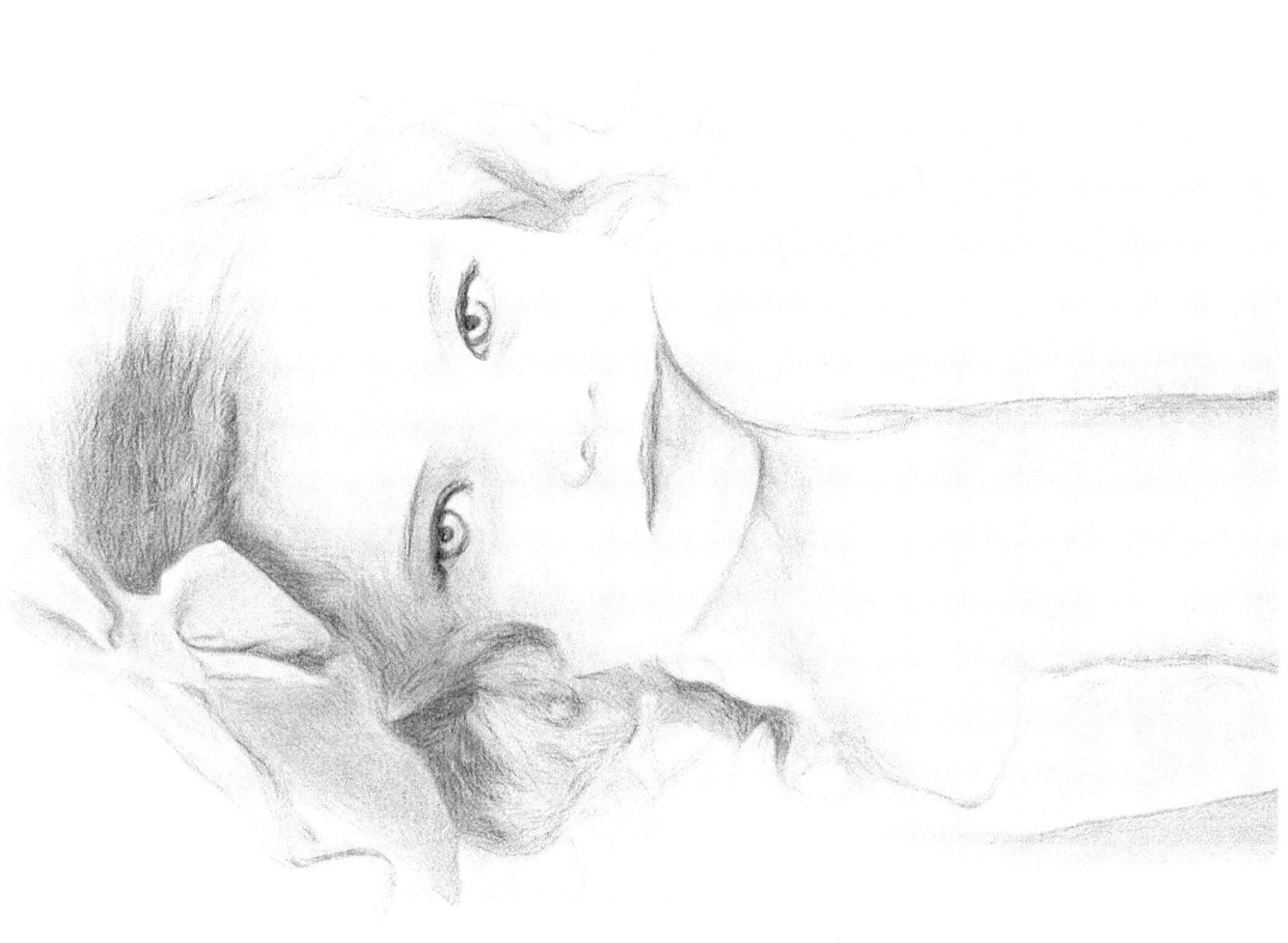

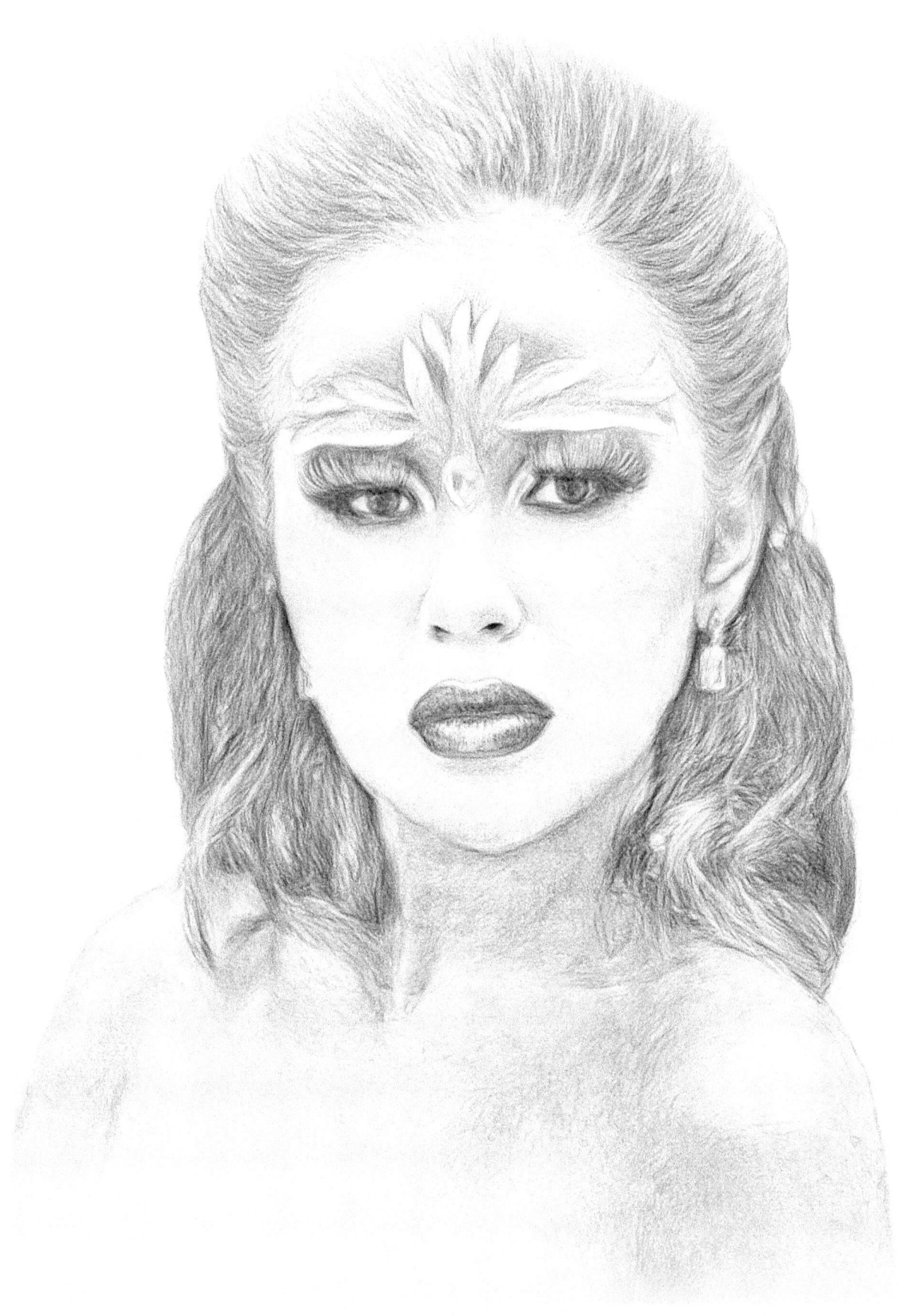

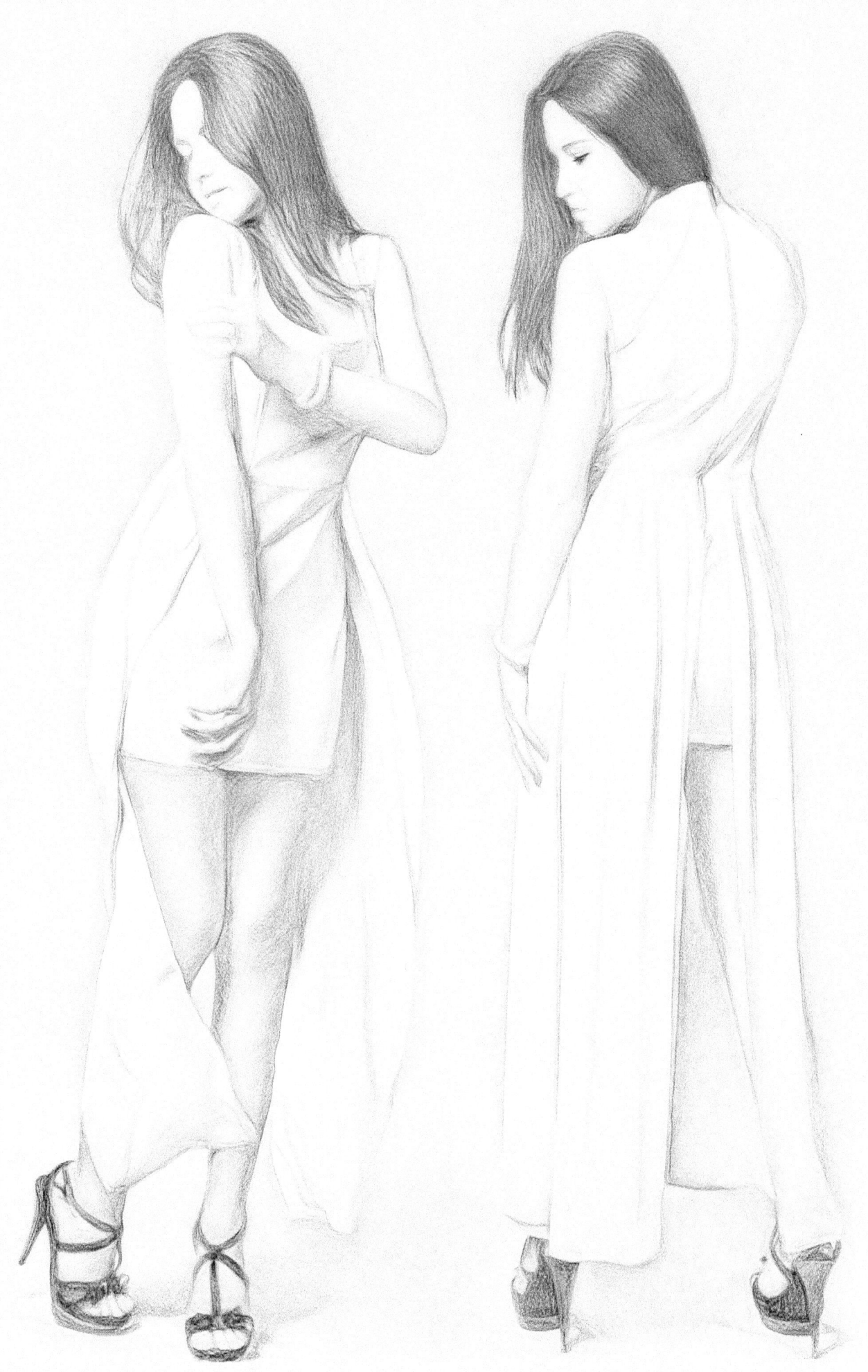

Part 2 – Deshading Style

I also do experiments. These illustrations were digitally captured by special photo processing and manual retouching. The effect is something between line art, photography and painting.

I named this style "Deshading" because I digitally remove the shading from the image, leaving only lines and motifs, no texture.

Your task now is to add your own "shading" in a painterly way. To color such illustrations, you can finally use markers (even gold or silver), or crayons and paints.

You can see more of these works in my book in the "Simply Coloring" series, Vol 3, "Flowers, Landscapes and Romantic Pictures ".

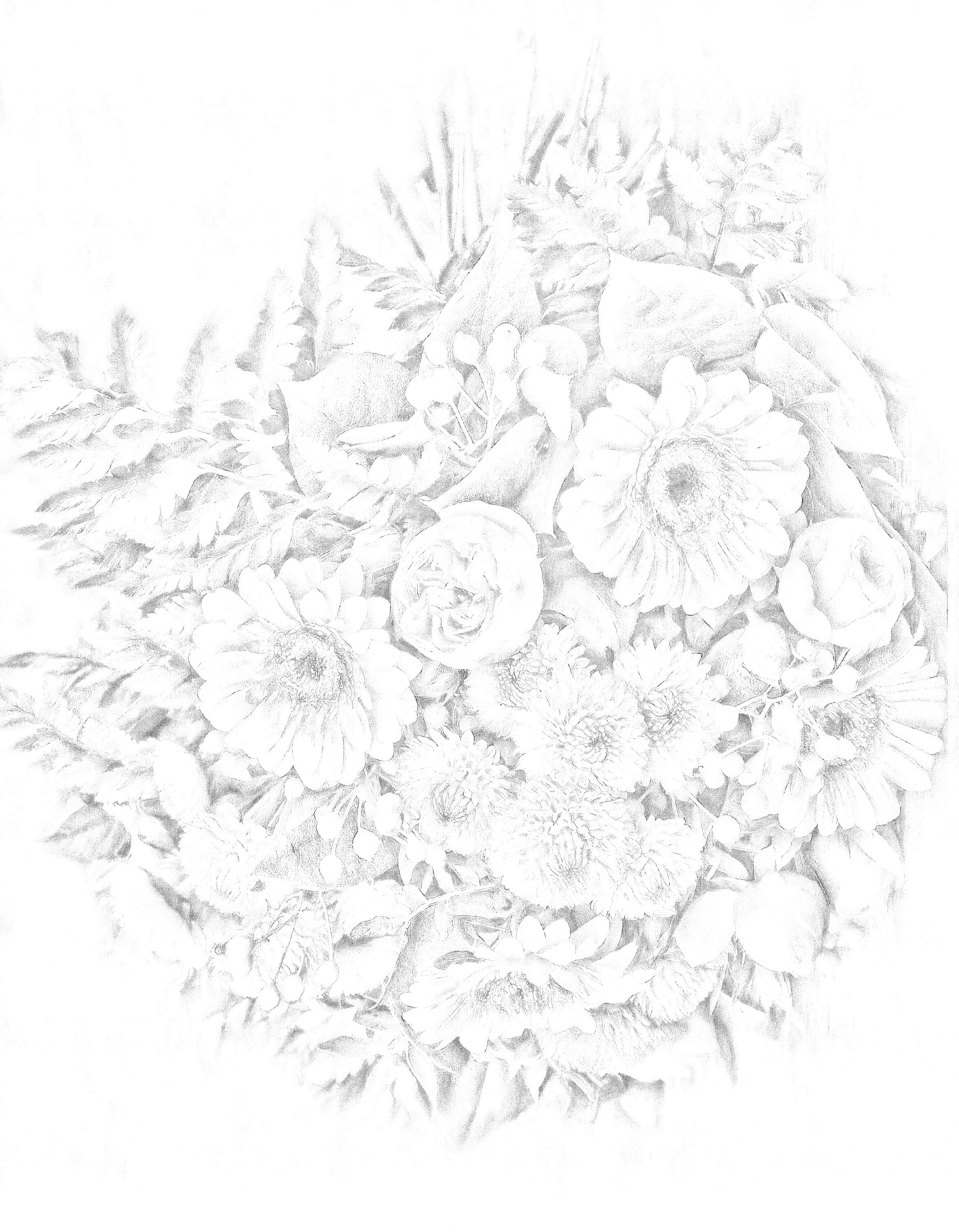

Part 3 – Best Mix of Flowers (for Beginners)

This section contains a selection of photos of delightful flowers from my previous grayscale coloring pages.

You also get 2 variants: with more contrast (this one), easy to color for beginners, and with low contrast (for advanced artists and if you want to use watercolors).

If the image is easy to paint or color then only one medium contrast version is available.

* * *

This part includes a more contrasting version.

I always get questions like: how to color such dark photos?
I have included extensive advice in my Guide.

And a quick advice is this: do not use watercolors because they are too transparent. But even black photo can be changed to saturated blue or yellow **if you use opaque paints (opaque acrylic paints or oil paints)**.

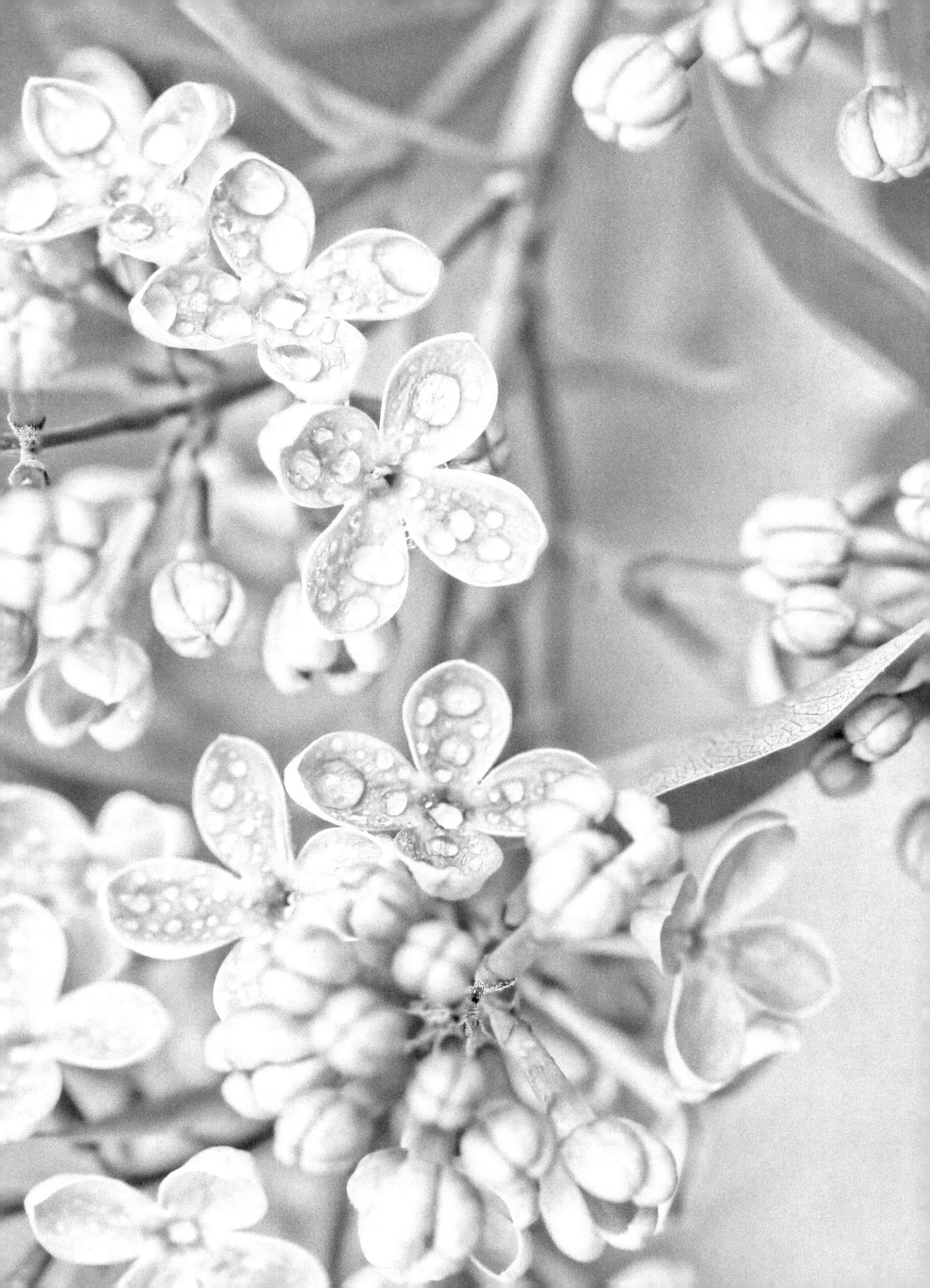

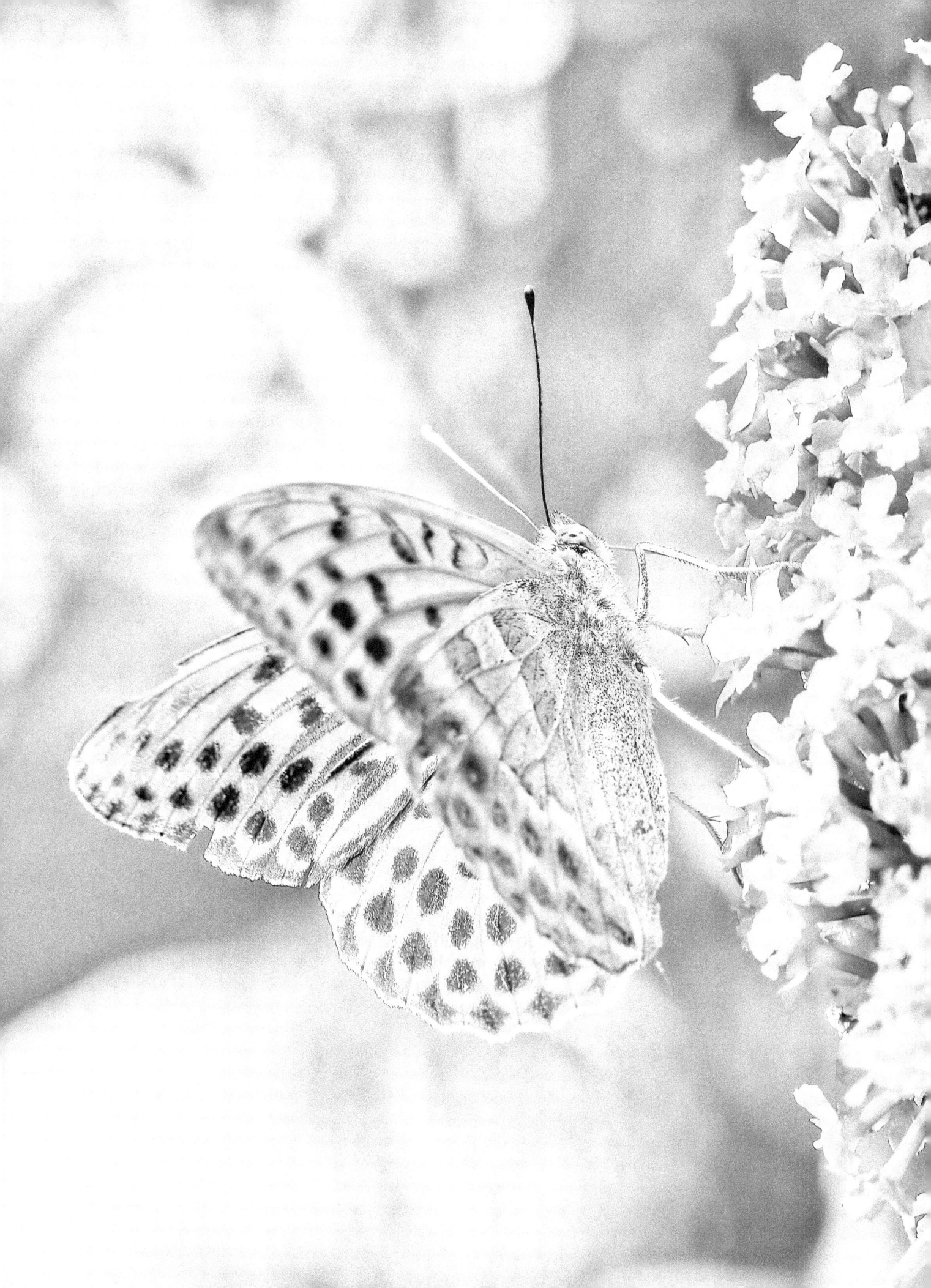

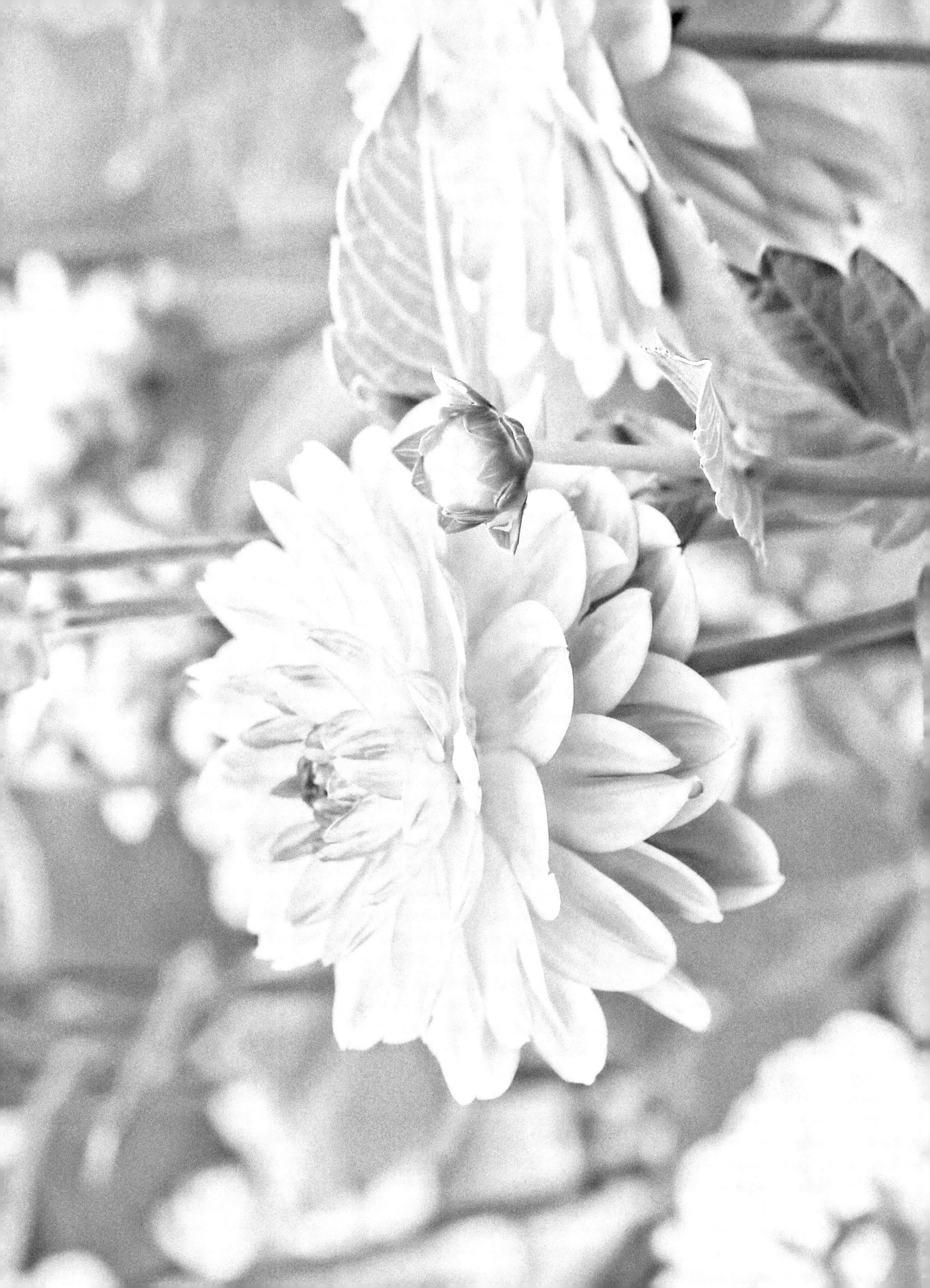

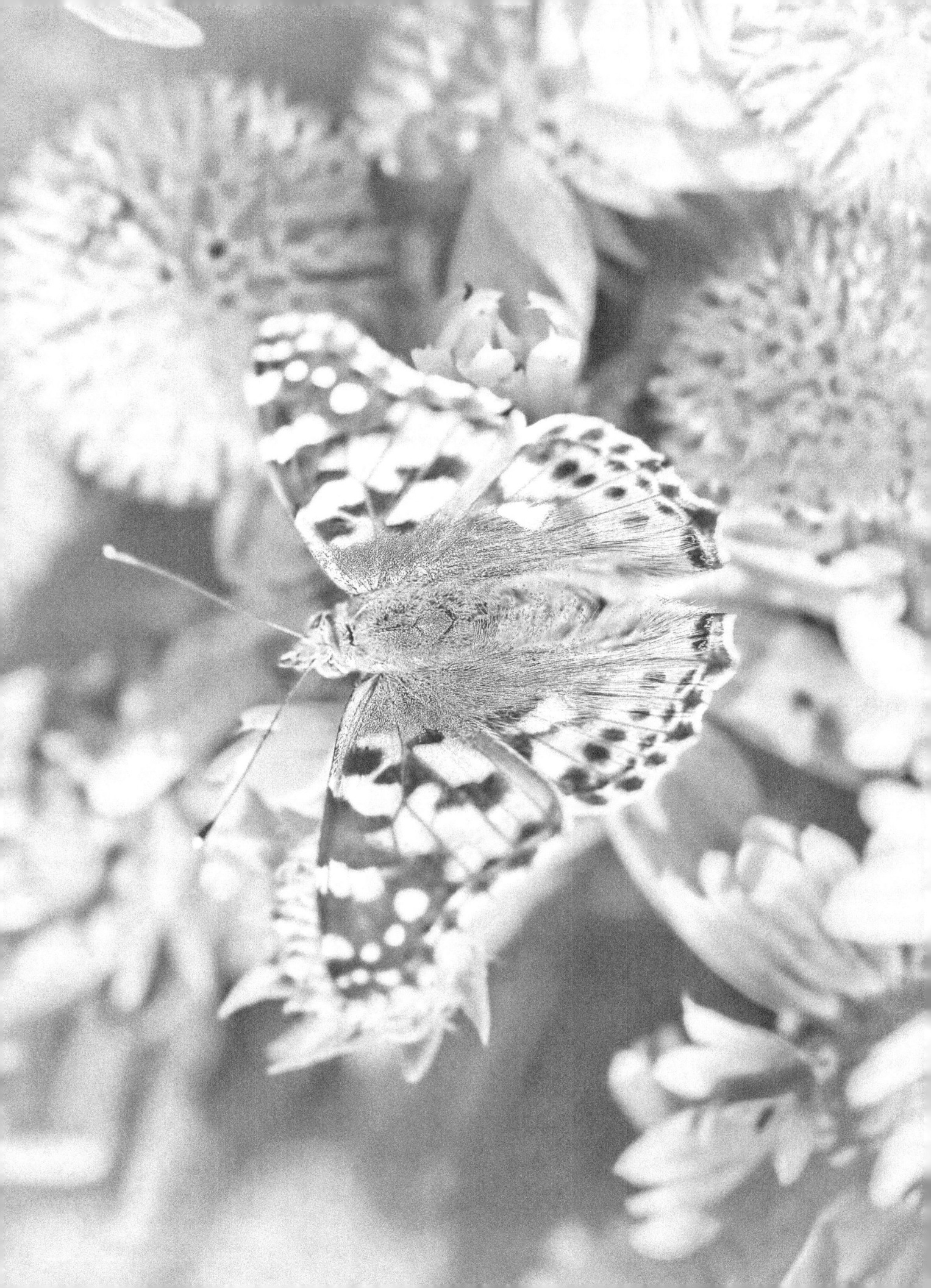

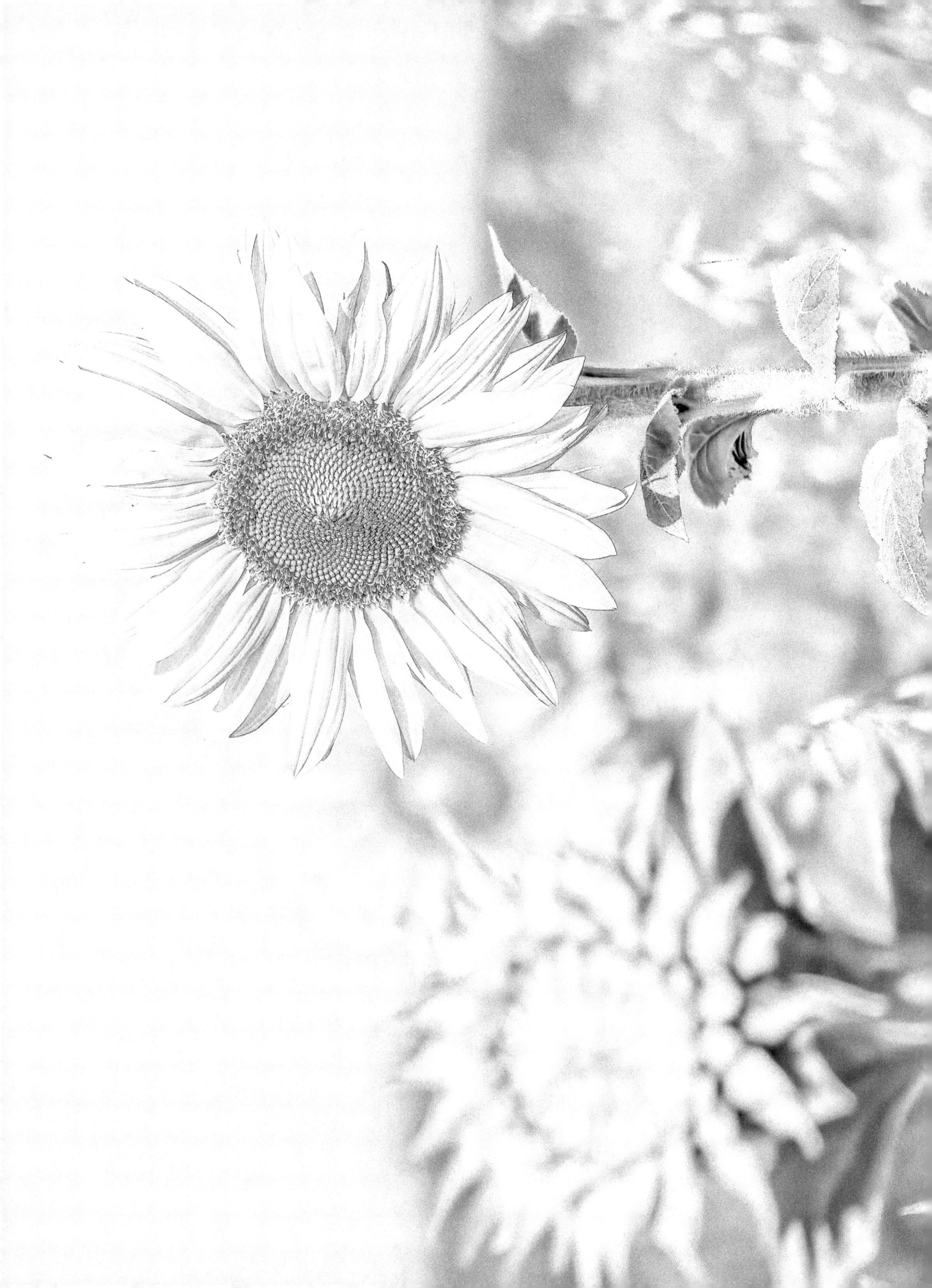

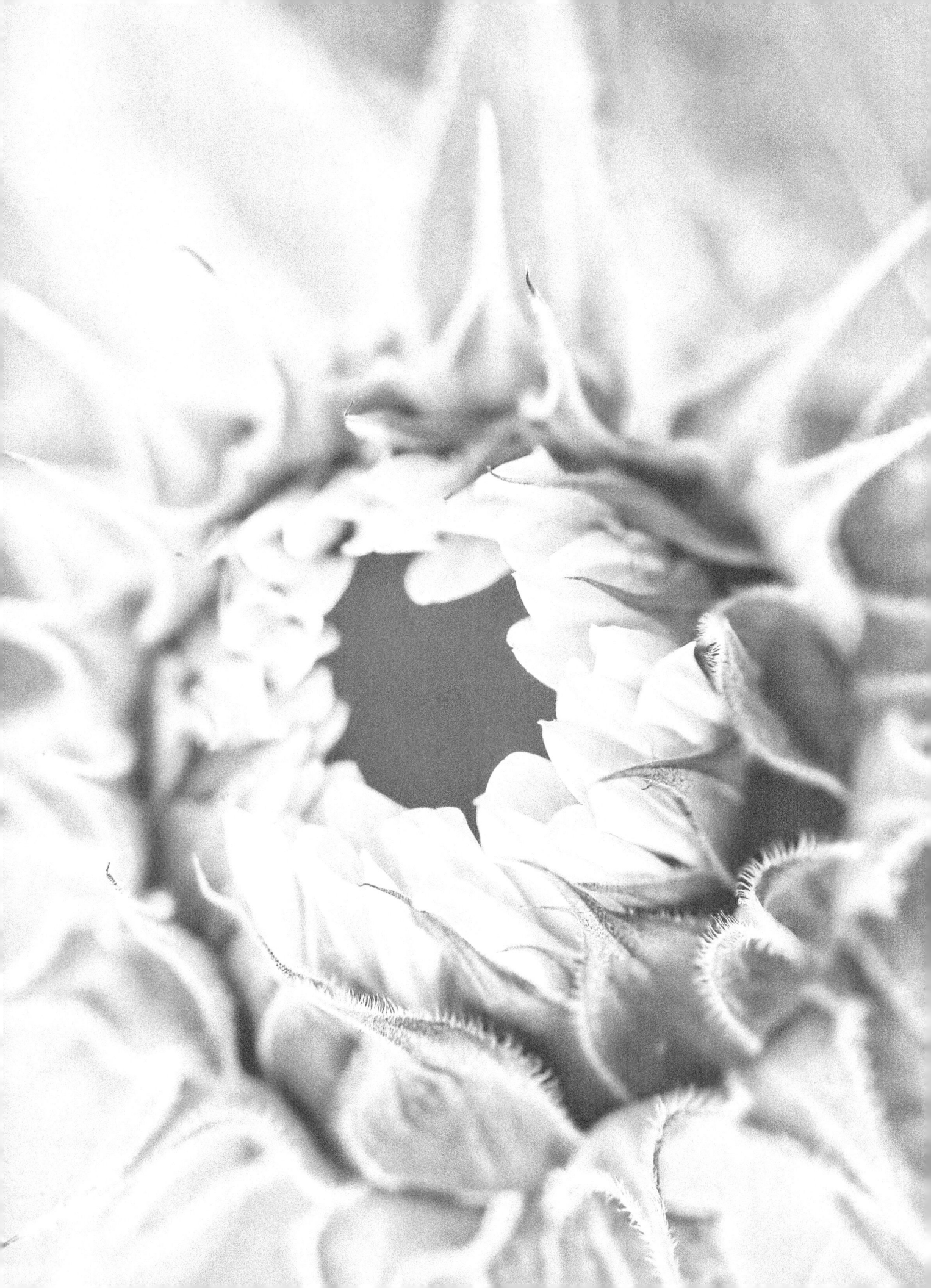

Artwork by / Œuvre par

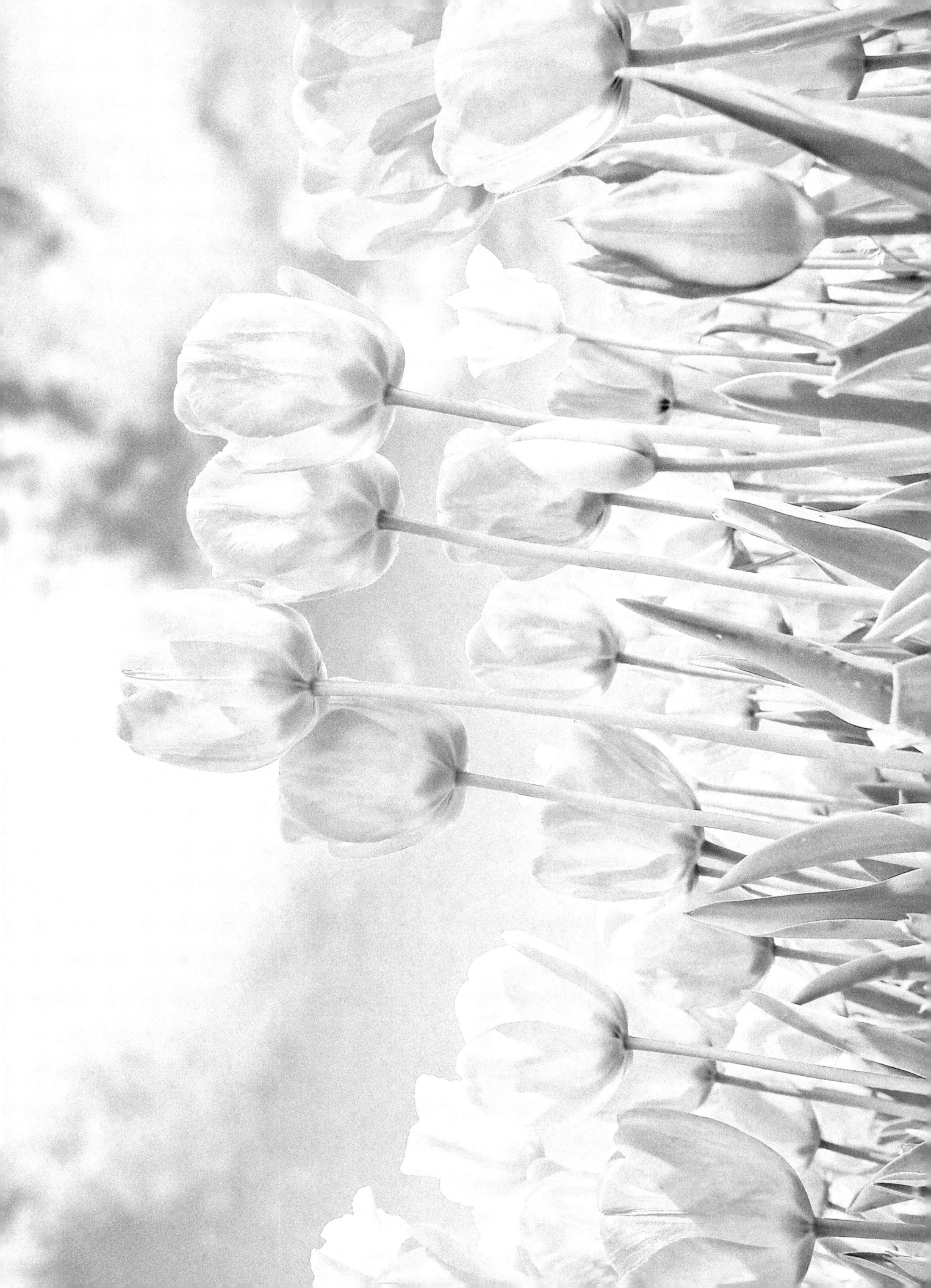

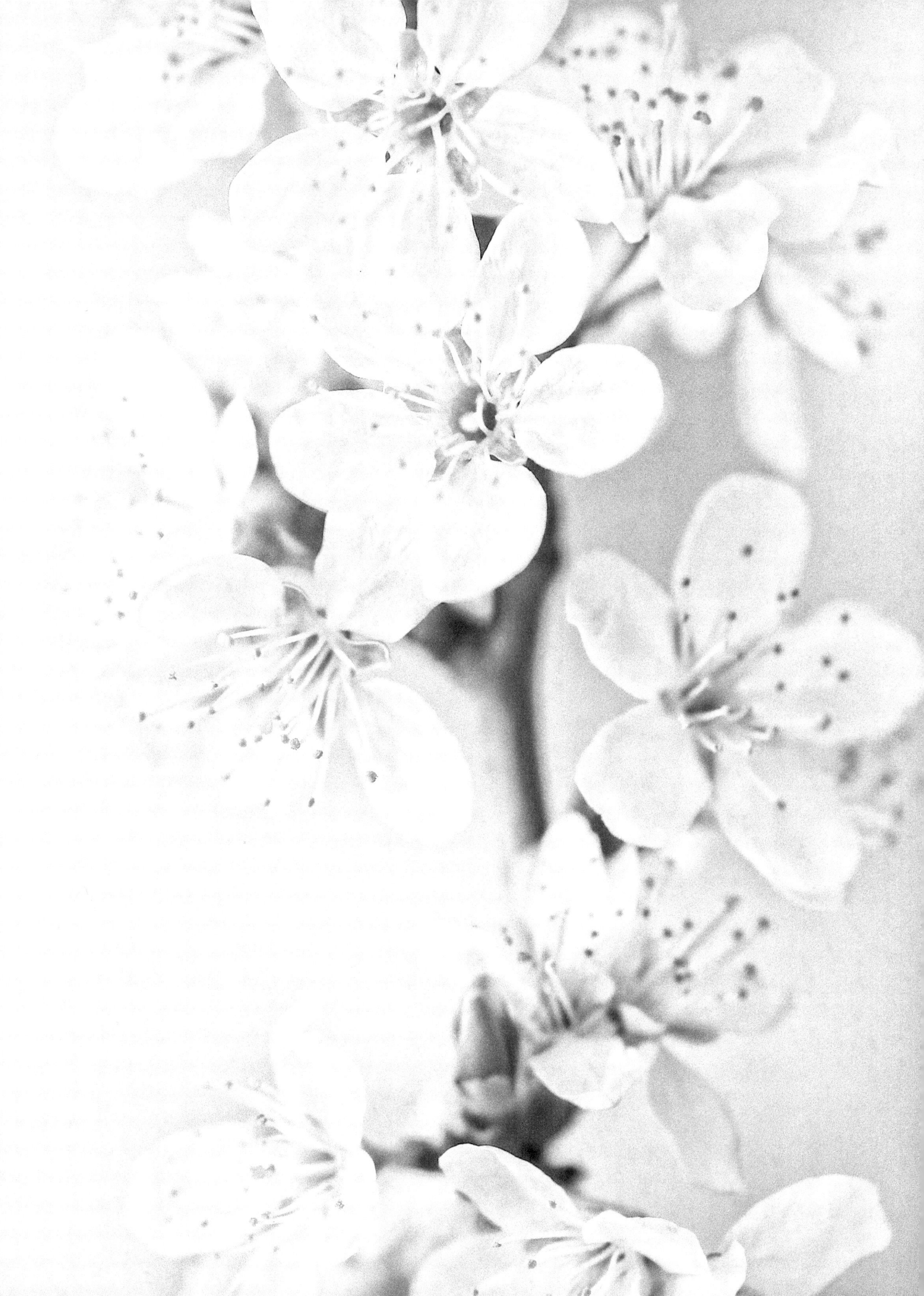

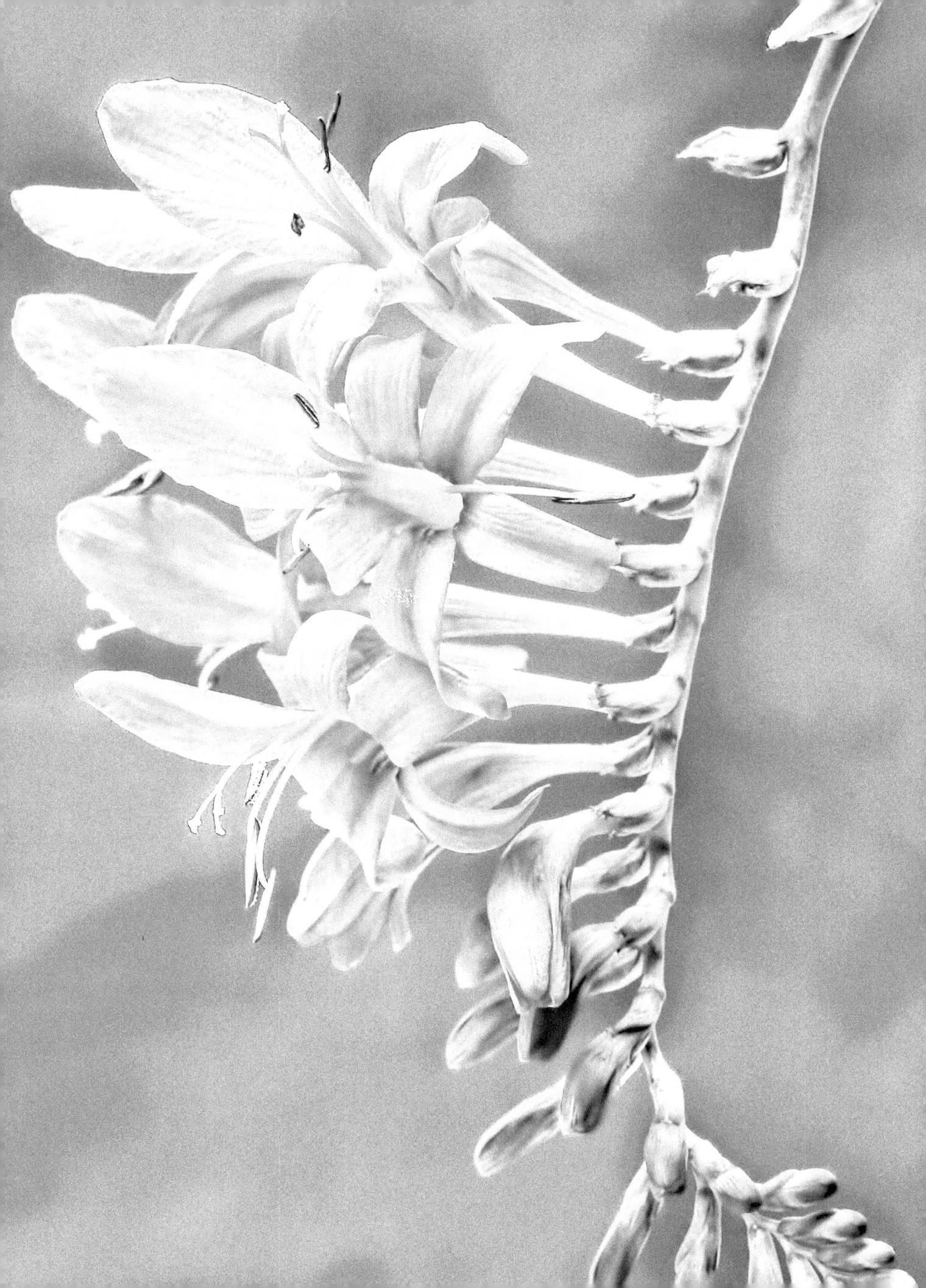

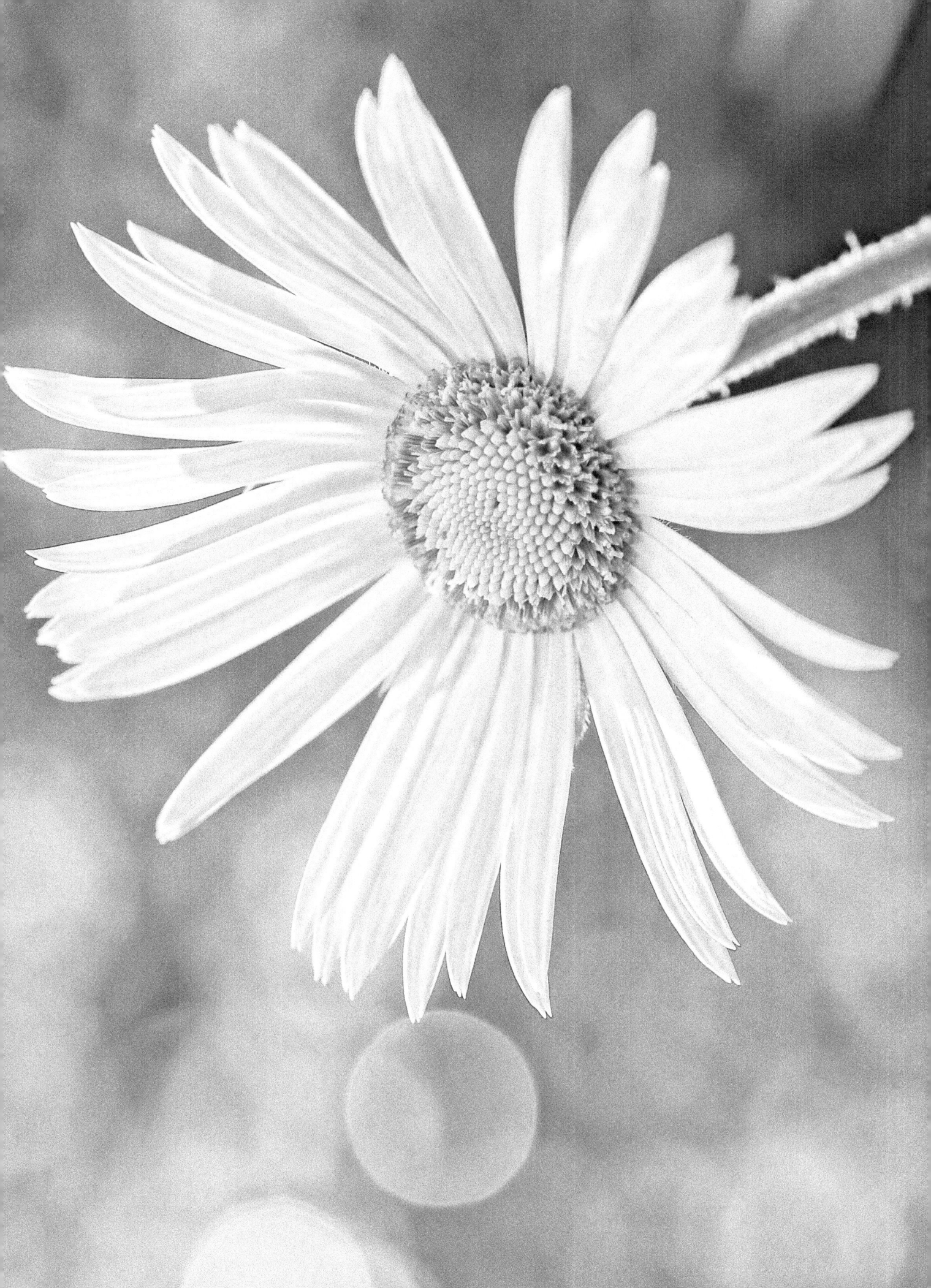

Artwork by / Œuvre par

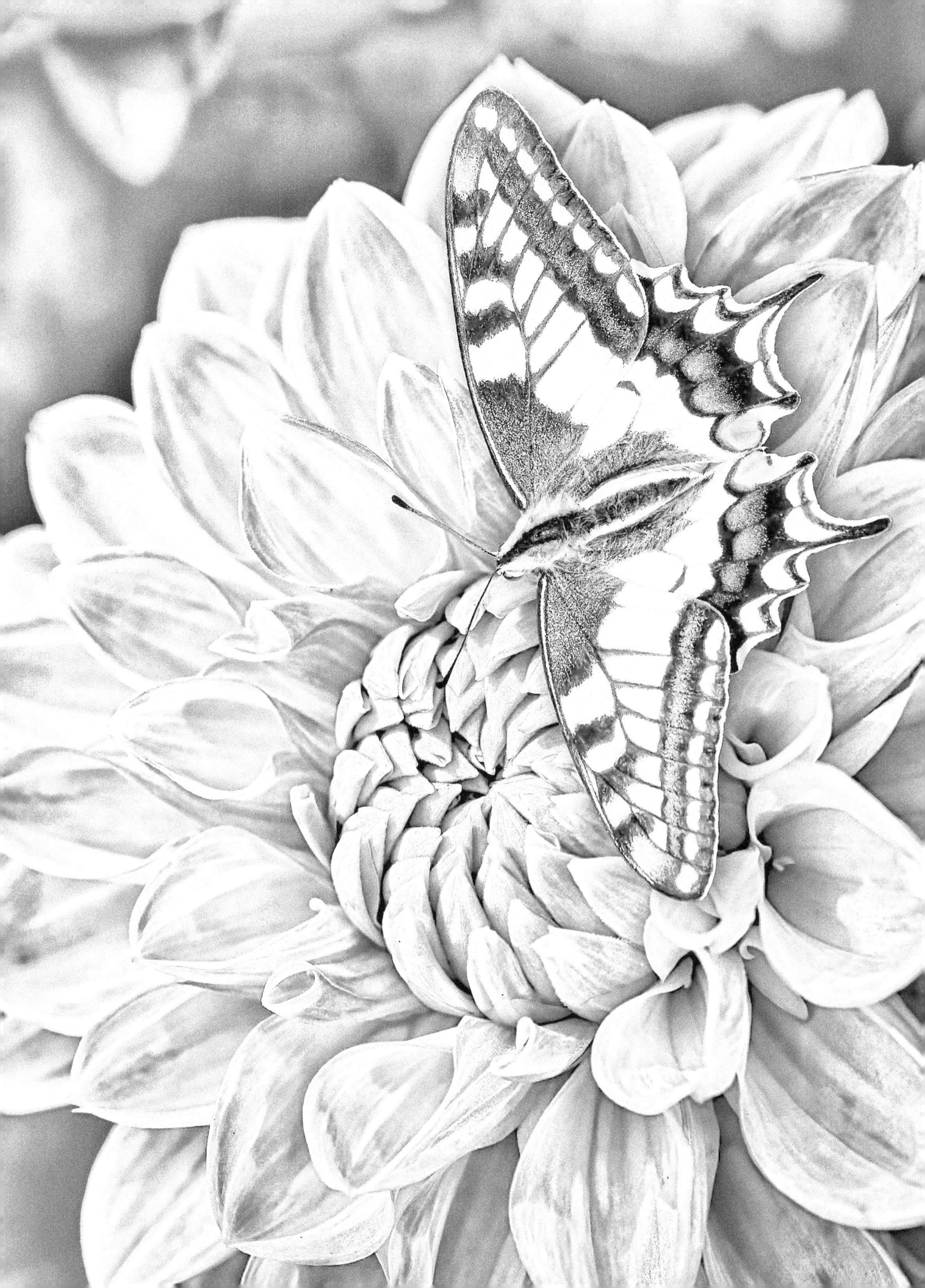

Artwork by / Œuvre par

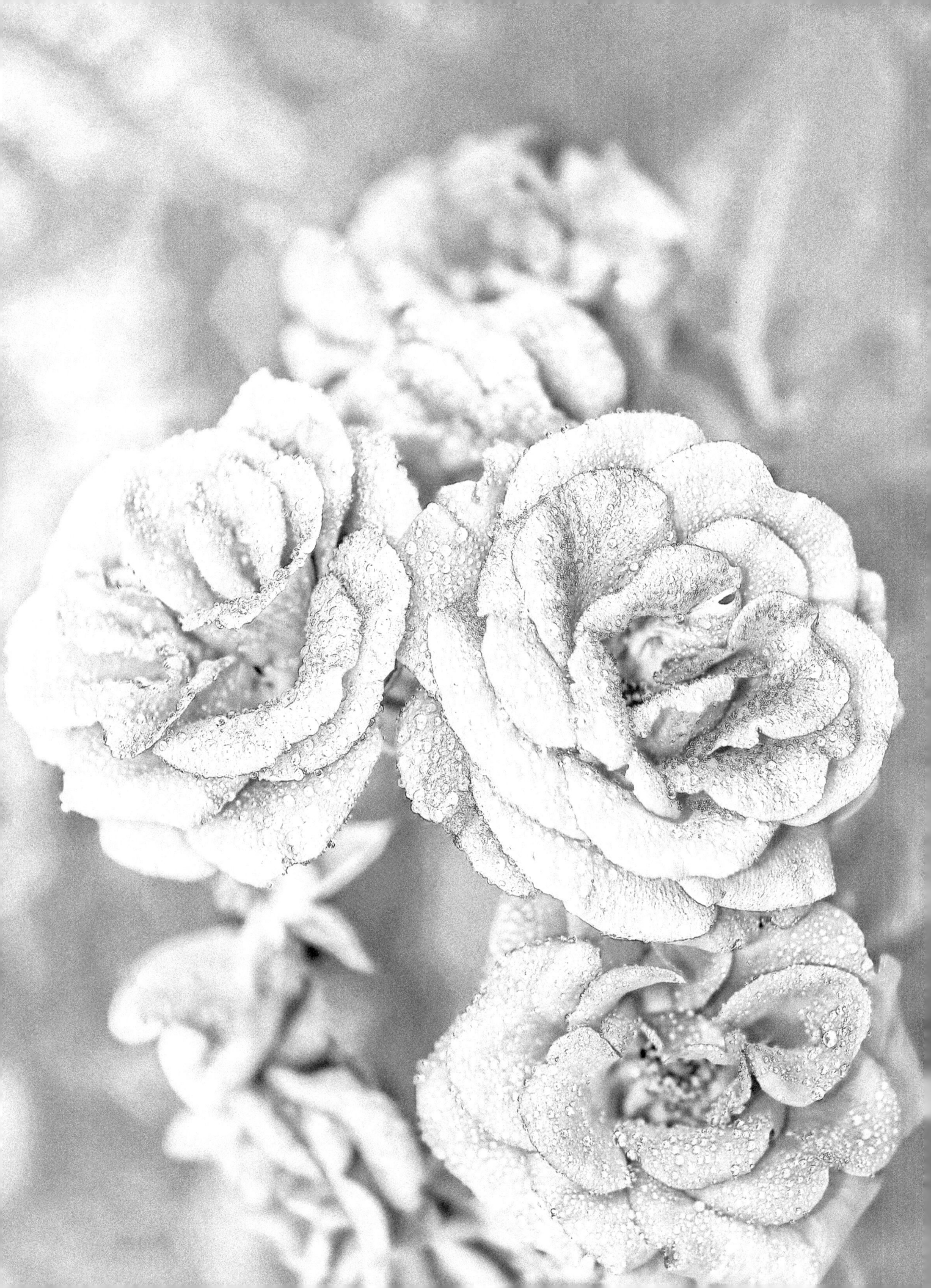

Artwork by / Œuvre par

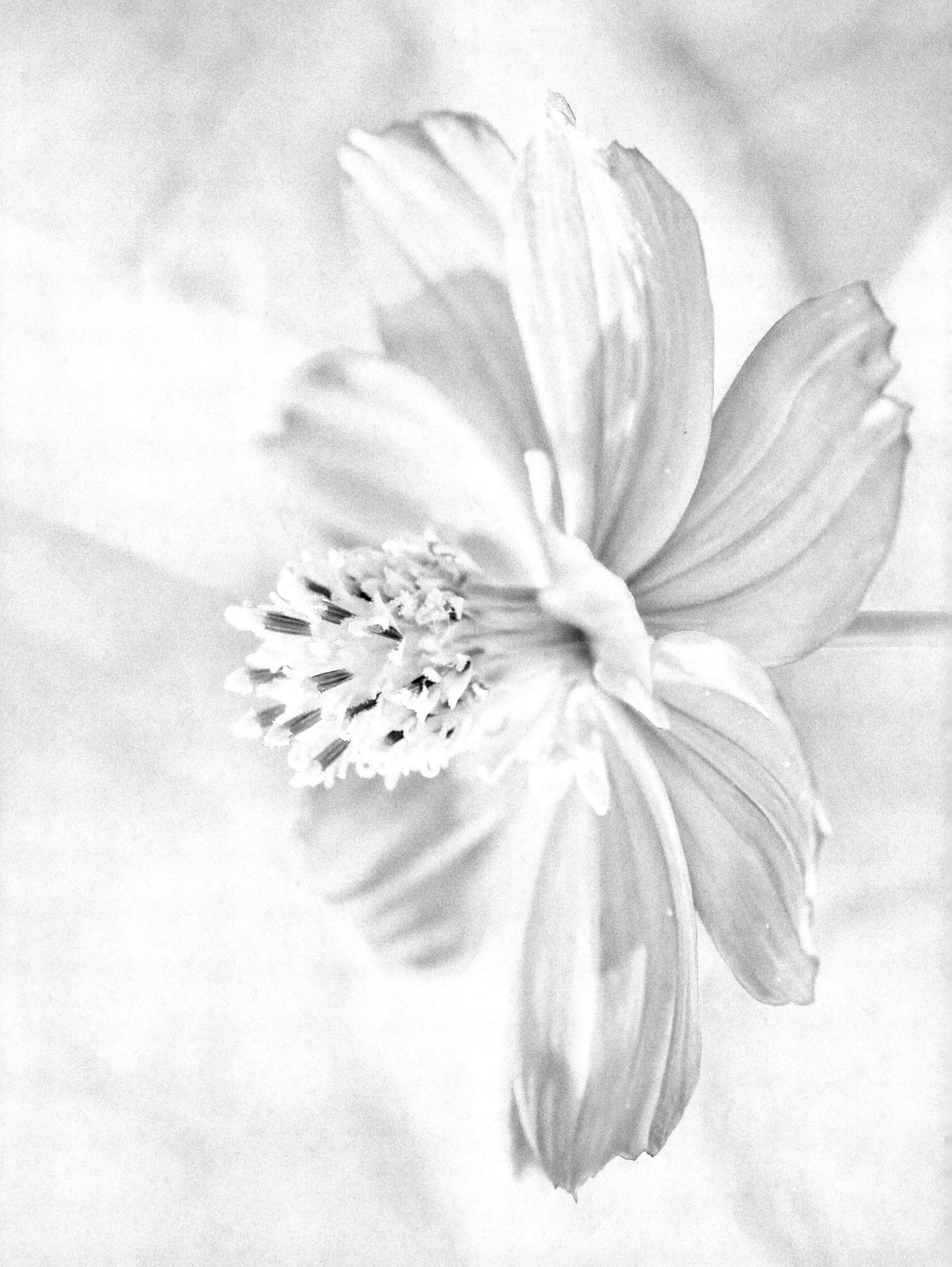

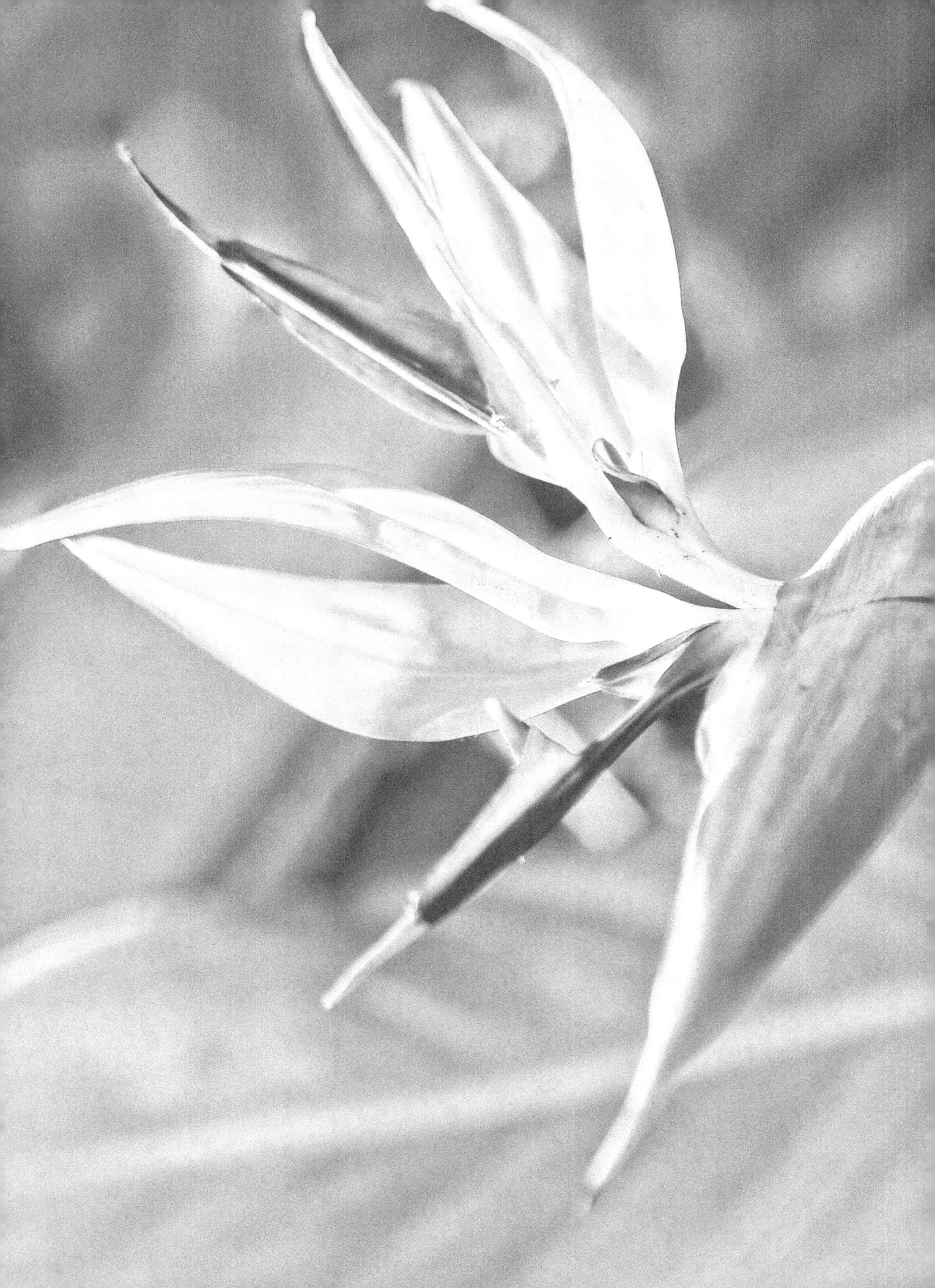

Artwork by/l'Œuvre par

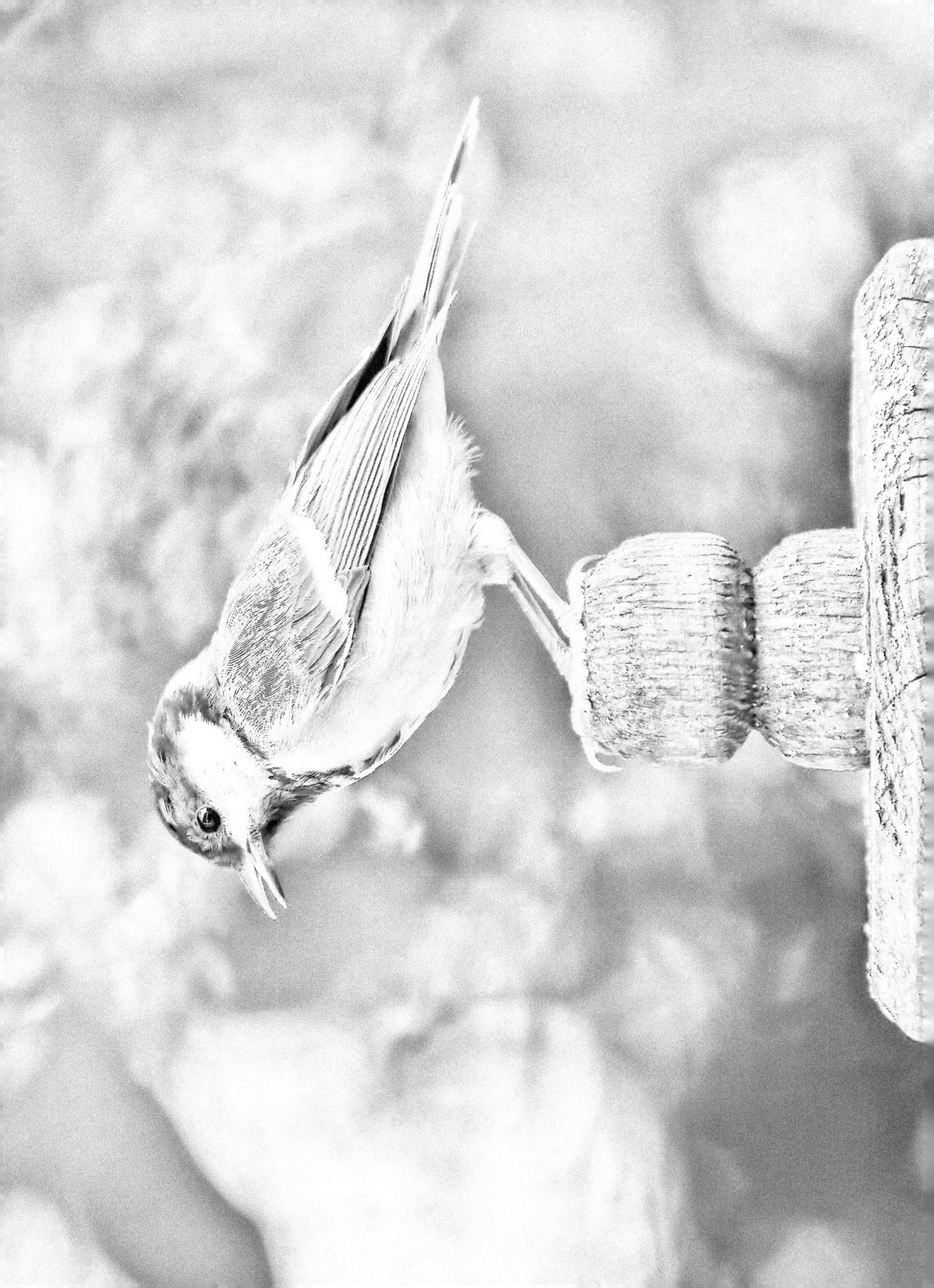

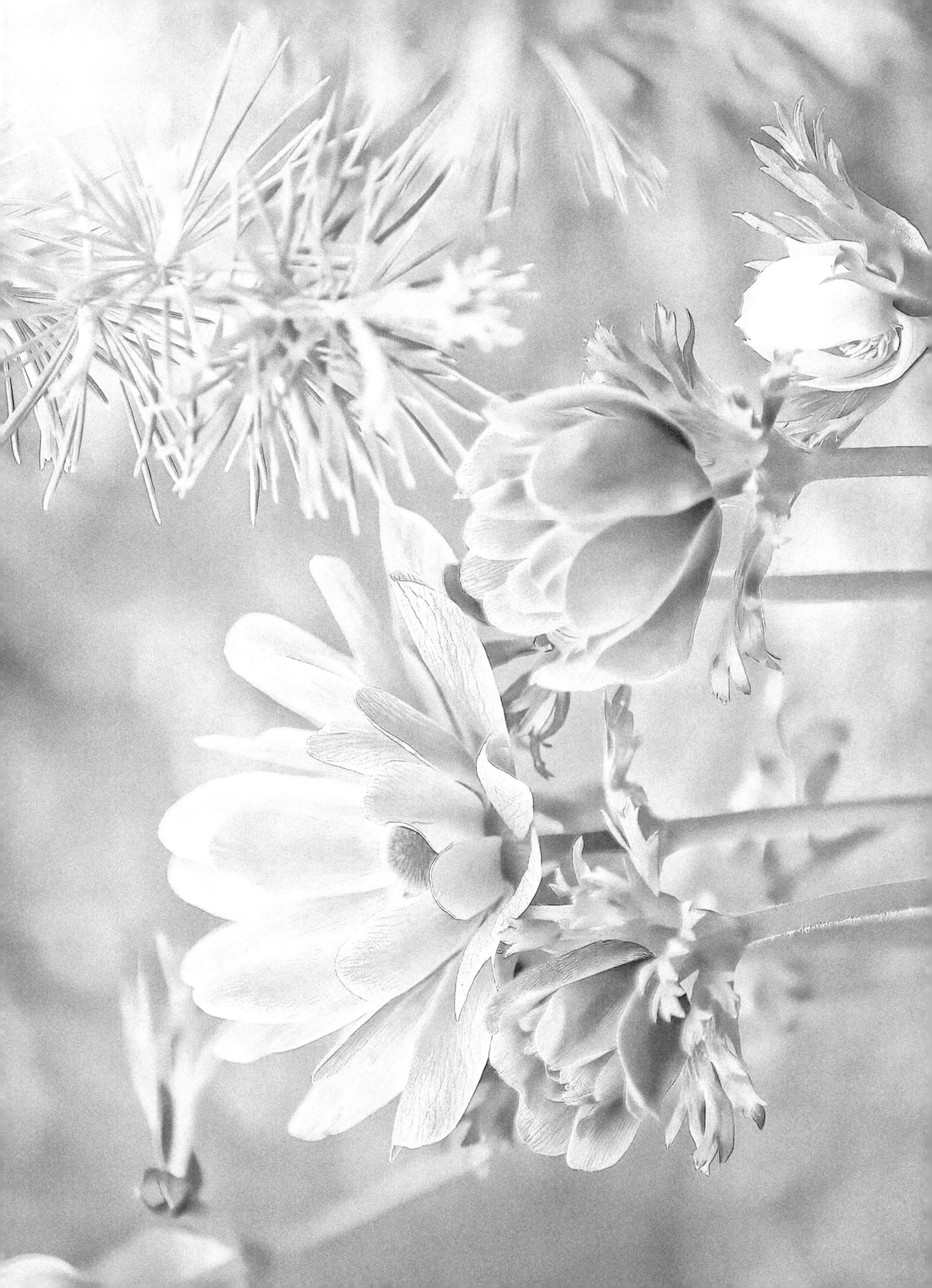

Part 4 – Various Pictures (For Beginners)

My version of Mona Lisa by Leonardo Da Vinci has been digitally restored and remastered using the latest methods (including my own AI - artificial intelligence), because I am also a programmer and I also create such applications.

The whole process took 18 hours of preliminary noise cleaning + a few more hours for manual retouching. I had to paint some parts from scratch, e.g. the sky, because the sky had too many scratches and cracks.

You have 4 versions at your disposal: 2 with high contrast and 2 with low contrast for advanced users (in further sections).

High-contrast versions are easy to color: just add colored pencils. The output image will be dark with some of its former glory.

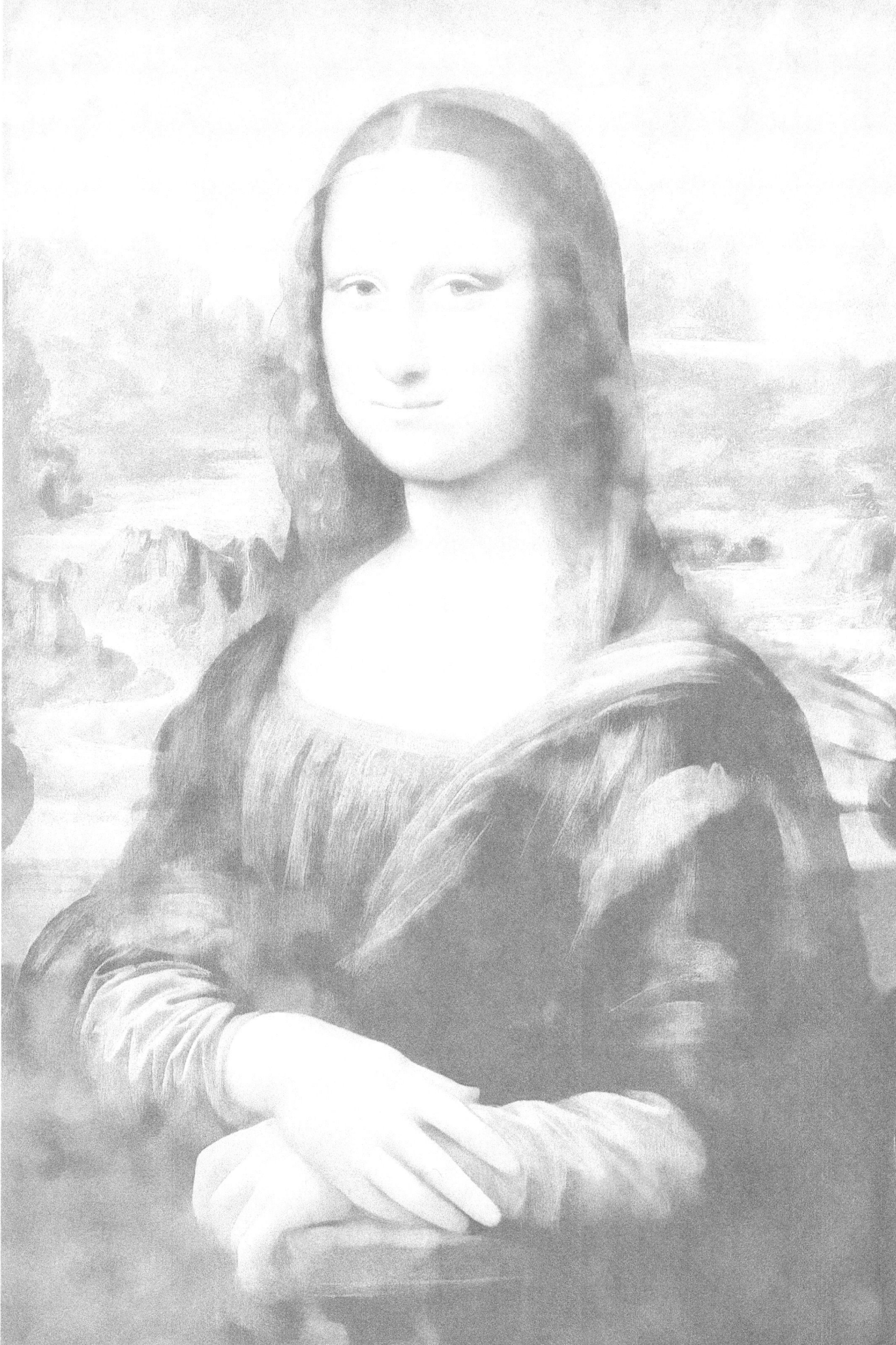

Artwork by Œuvre pais

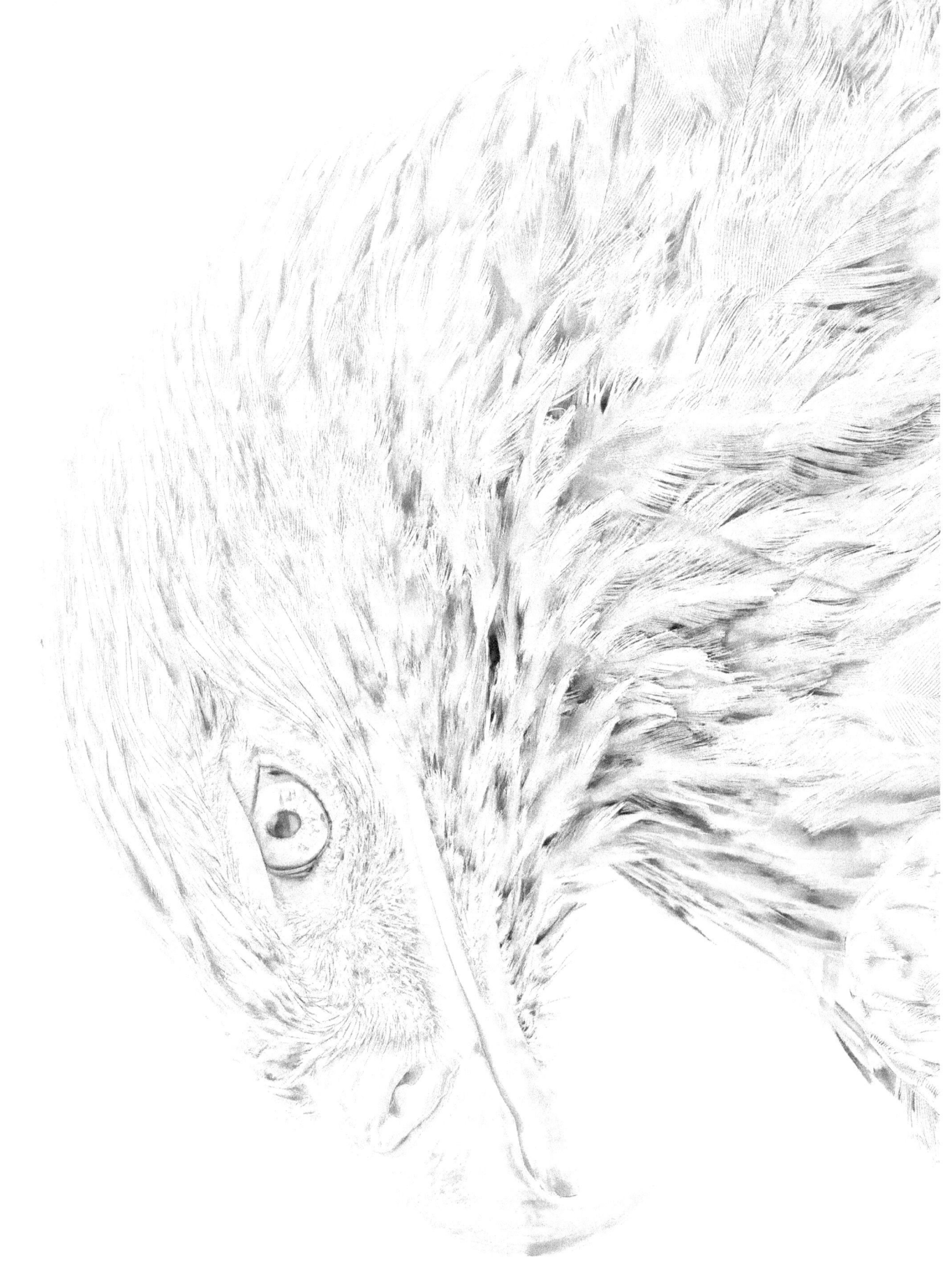

Artwork by l'Œuvre pur

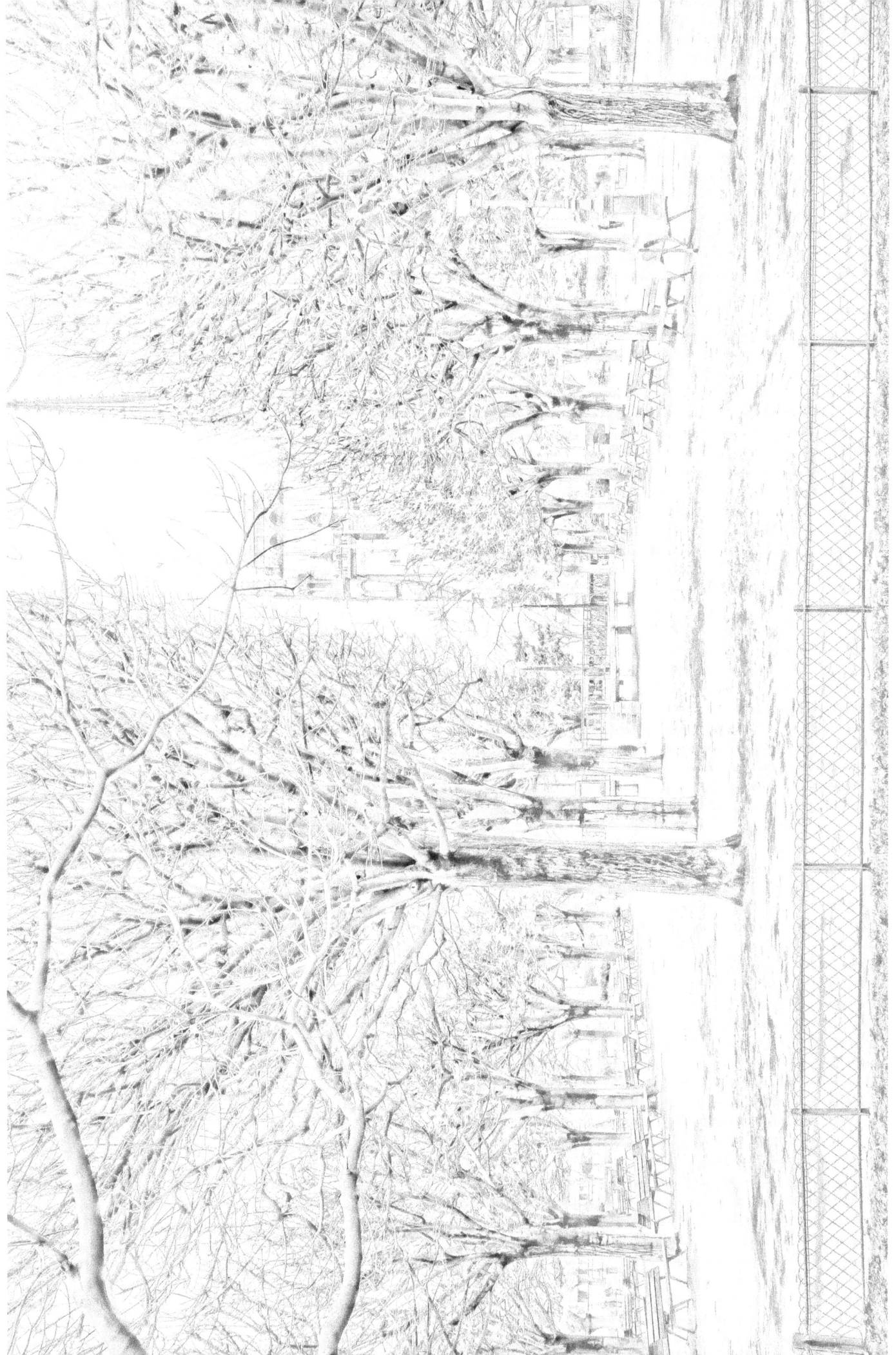

Paris, France, a Park

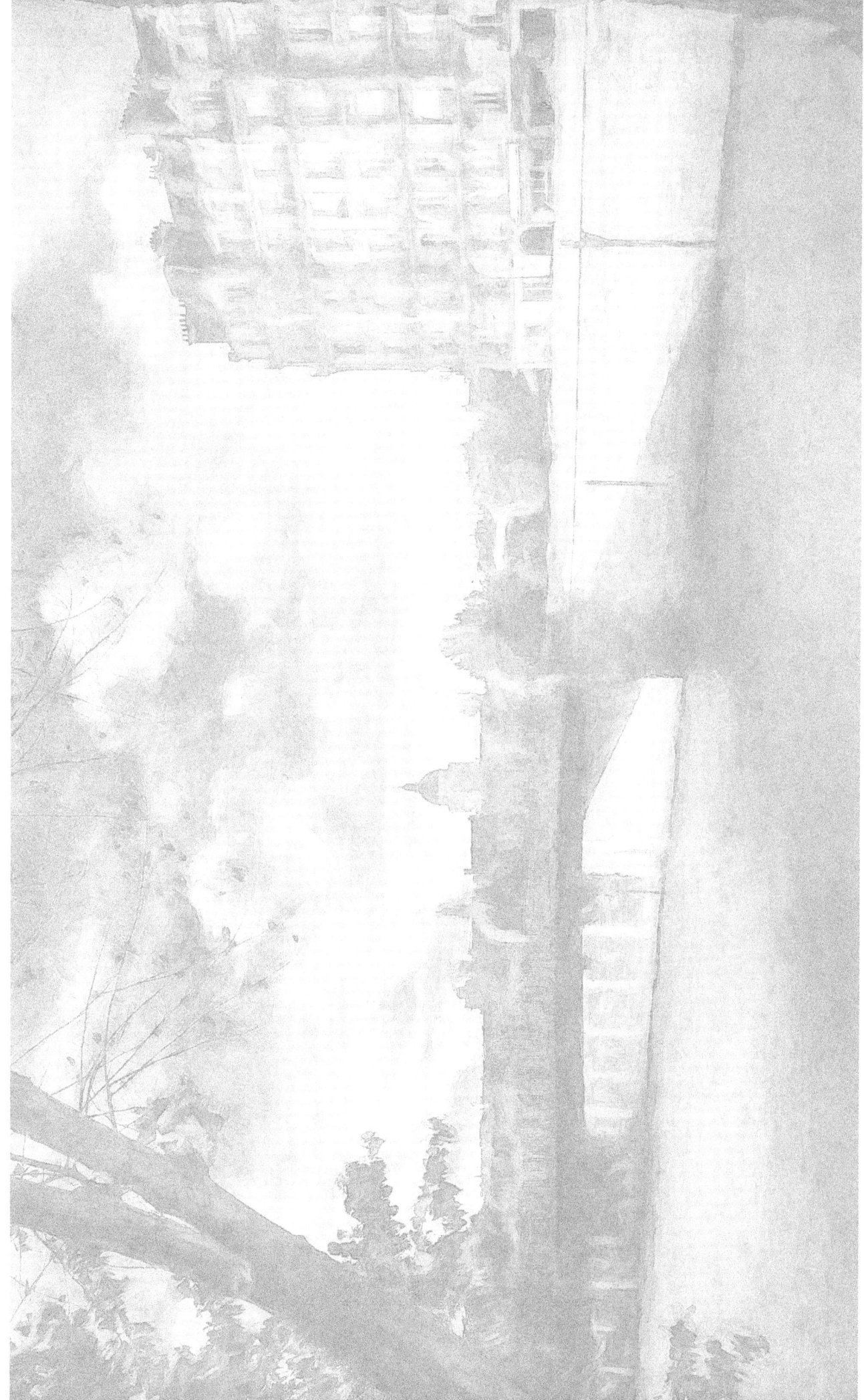

Paris, France, La Seine

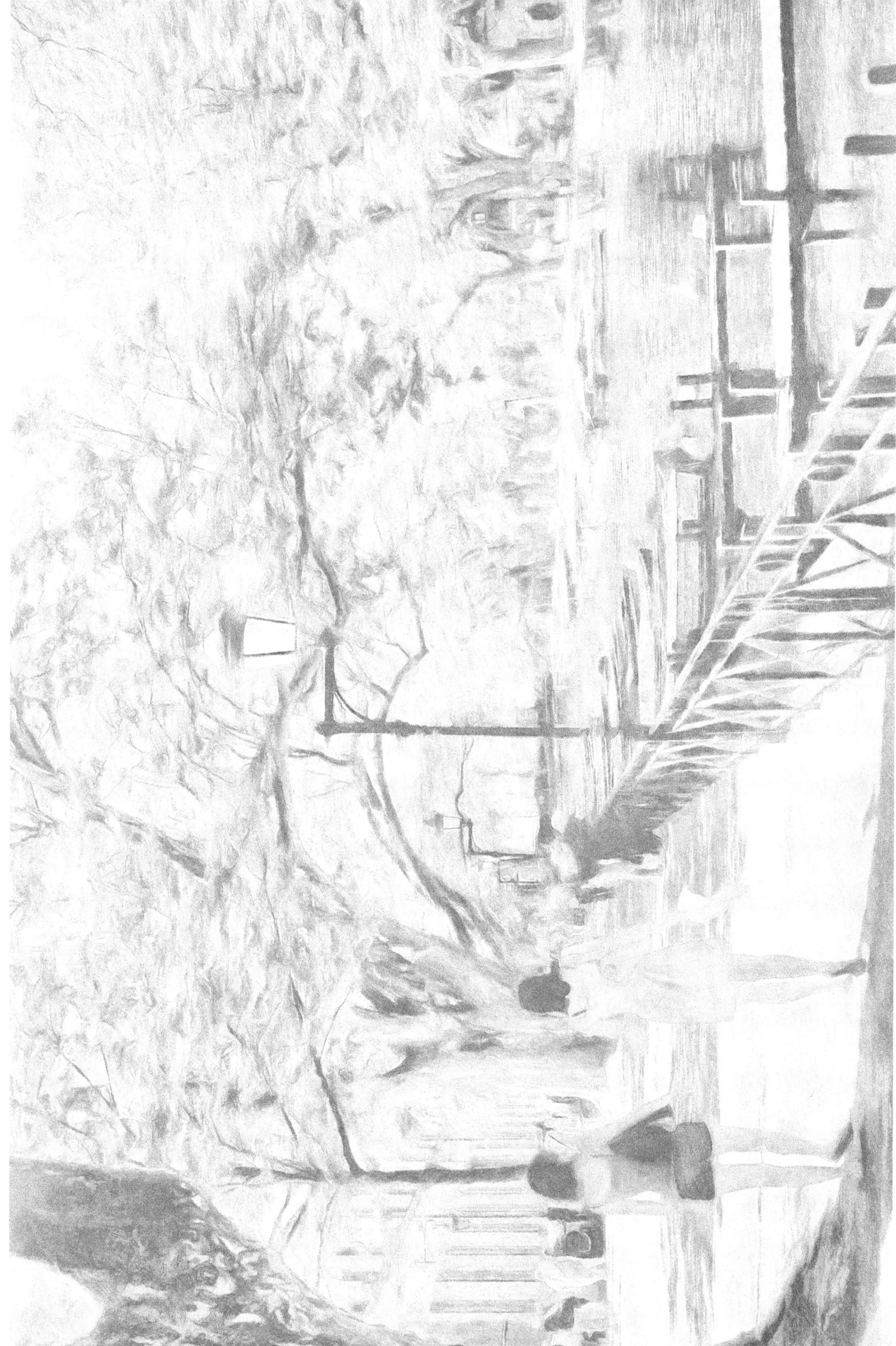

Part 5 – Living Drawings, Pencil

Low Contrast, for advanced artists

Tip: Before painting on low contrast pictures, cut out all the pages from the book (as shown in the Guide) and then use the high contrast tonal image as a reference image.

Just look at the high contrast reference image while painting on a low contrast sketch.

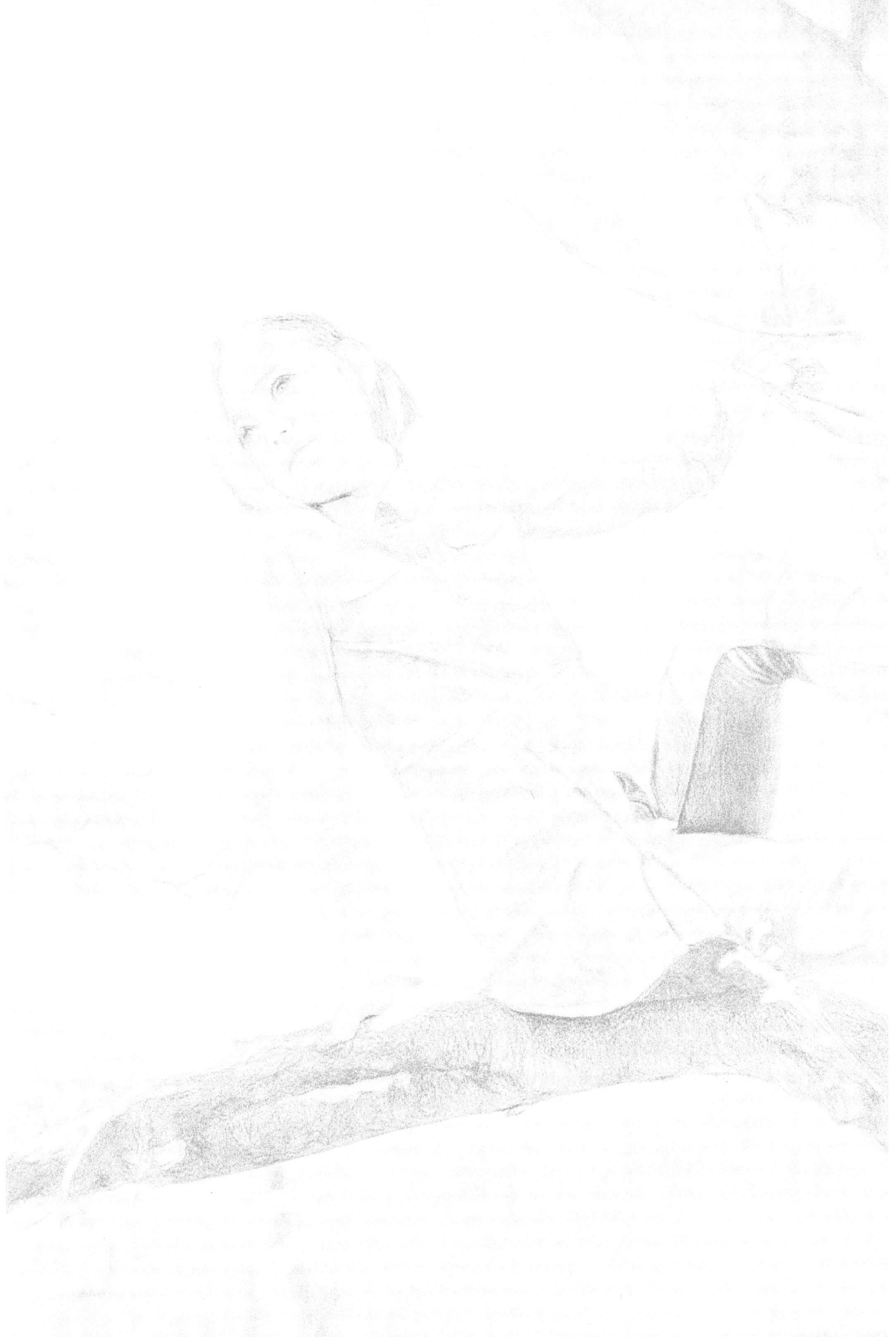

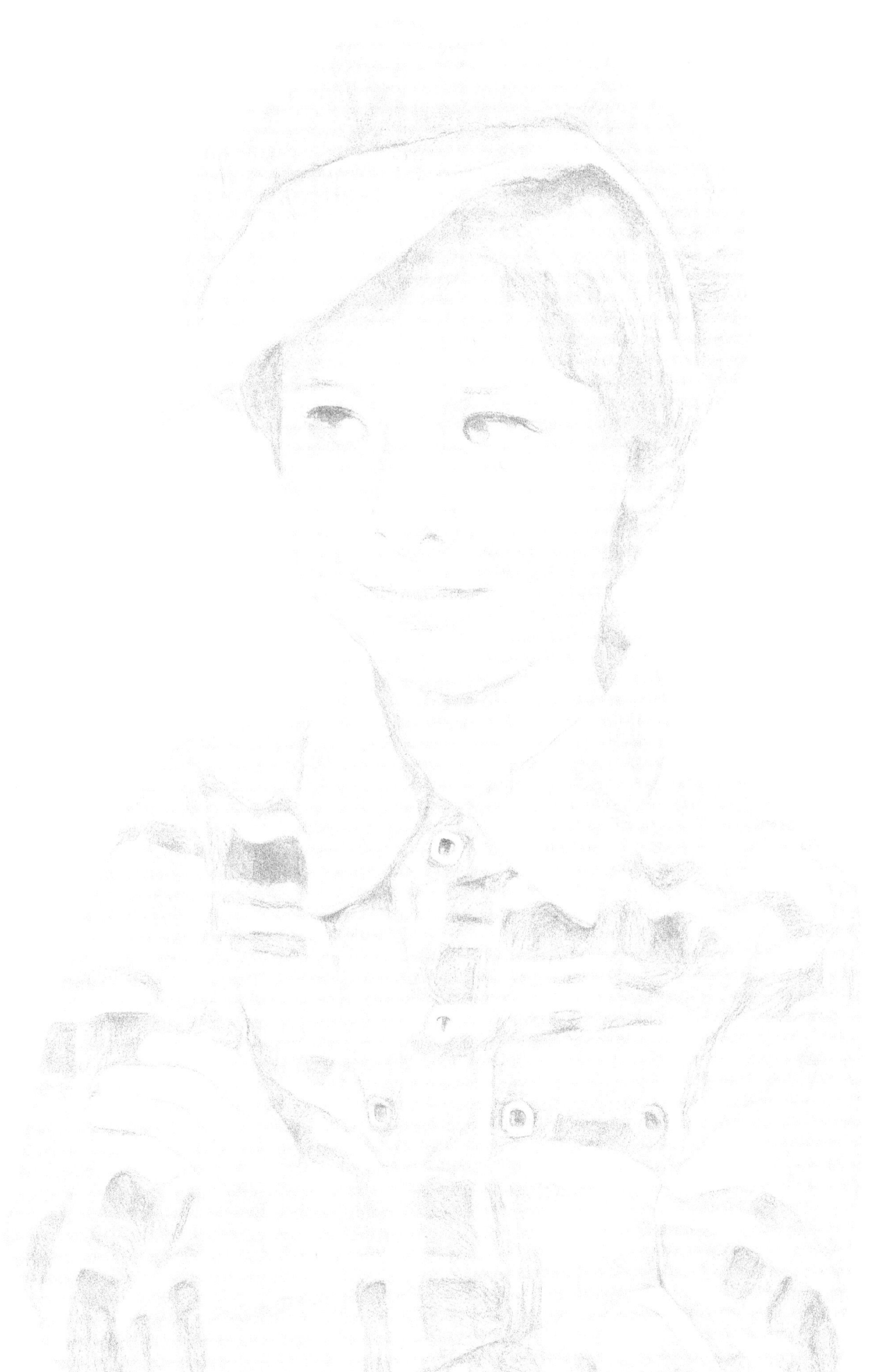

Artwork by / Œuvre par

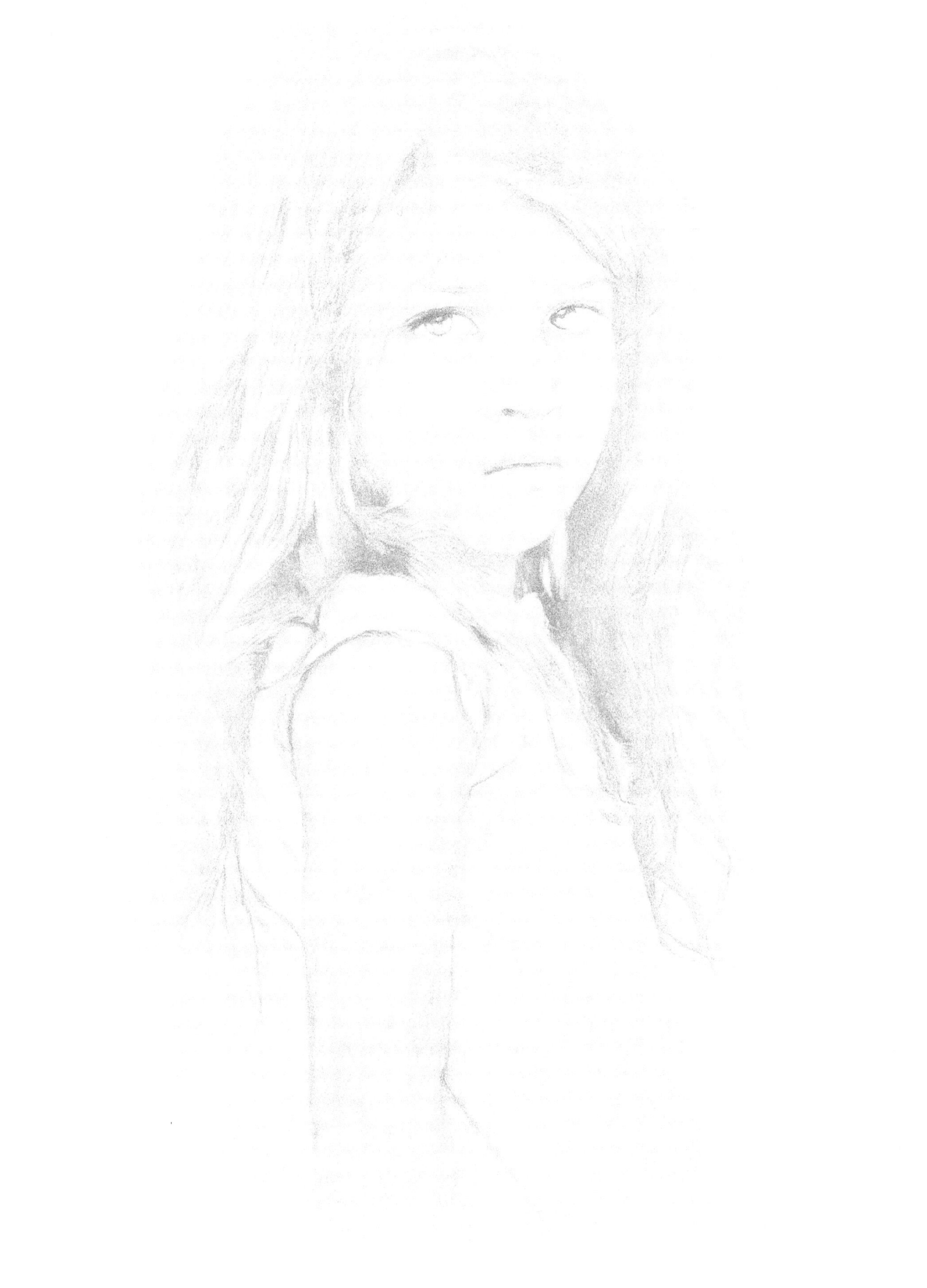

Artwork by / Œuvre par

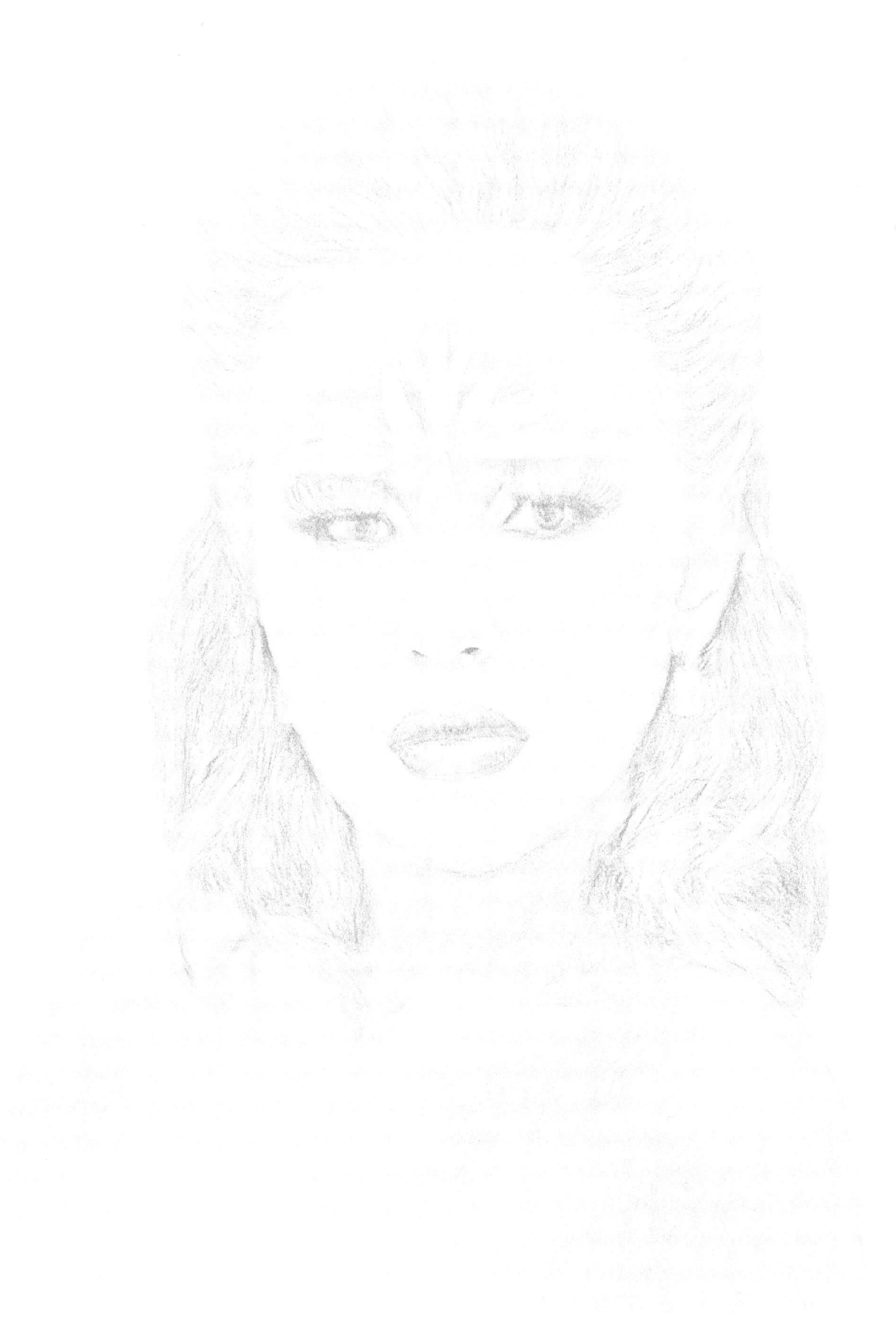

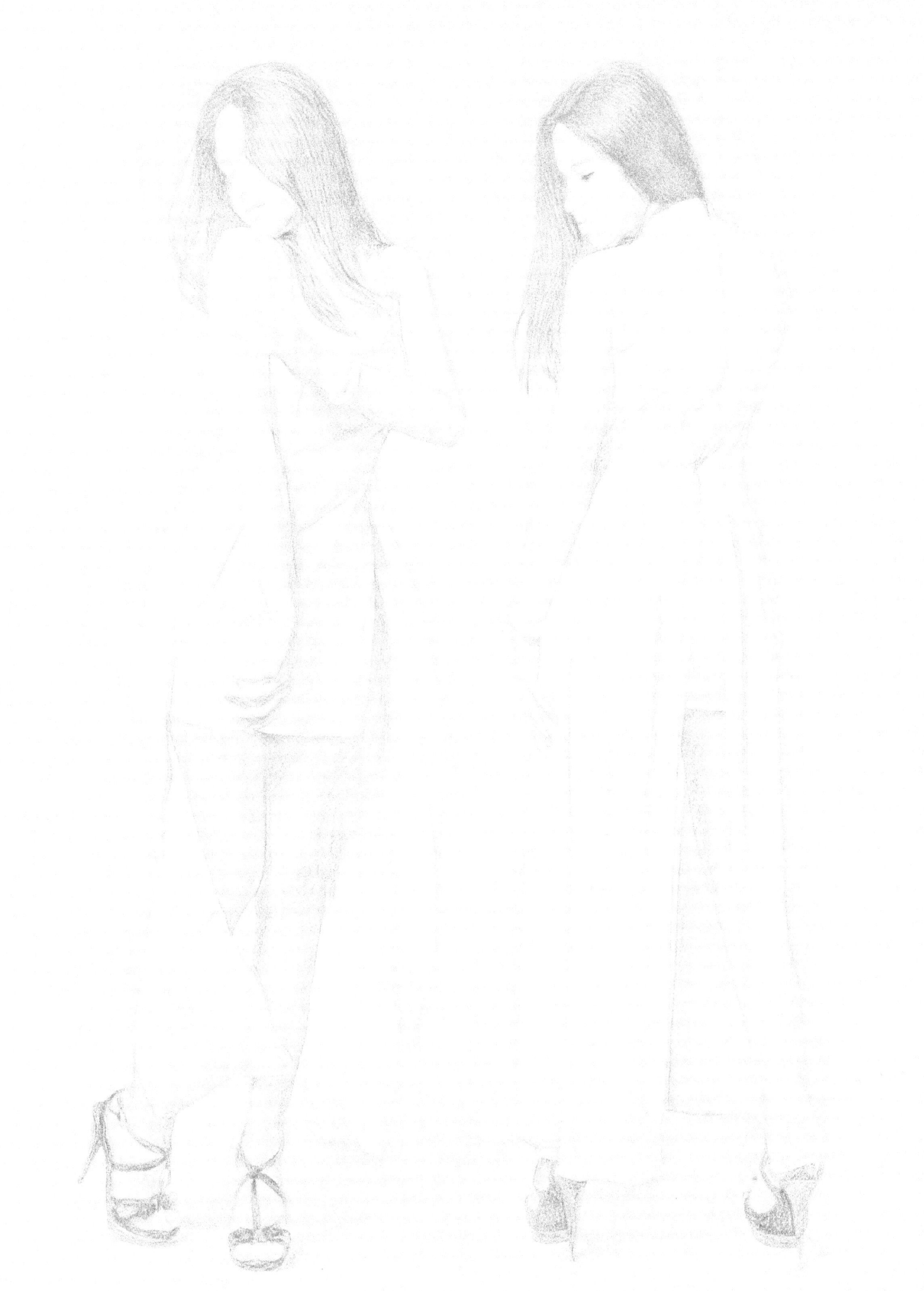

Part 6 – Best Mix of Flowers (Low Contrast)

To get the best effects, paining like, use a Hybrid Coloring way, described in my Guide.

* * *

I mean more advanced artists who are not content with coloring childish lines of easy shapes.

When I say "Low Contrast" or "Advanced" I mean different images that are bright or even very bright with less detail visible. The level of "lightening" can vary. That's why you will always find something for yourself.

You can use such a picture as a sketch for your own paintings, on which you can paint your own motifs, or paint almost the entire picture from scratch (using opaque paints) leaving only the main motif from my print, and then adding your own shapes, e.g. rainbow, lights and shadows, elves, spirals, circles, flowers, clouds etc.

I also mean that my painting may only be an inspiration for you, and you will paint something completely different on it. Like a real artist.

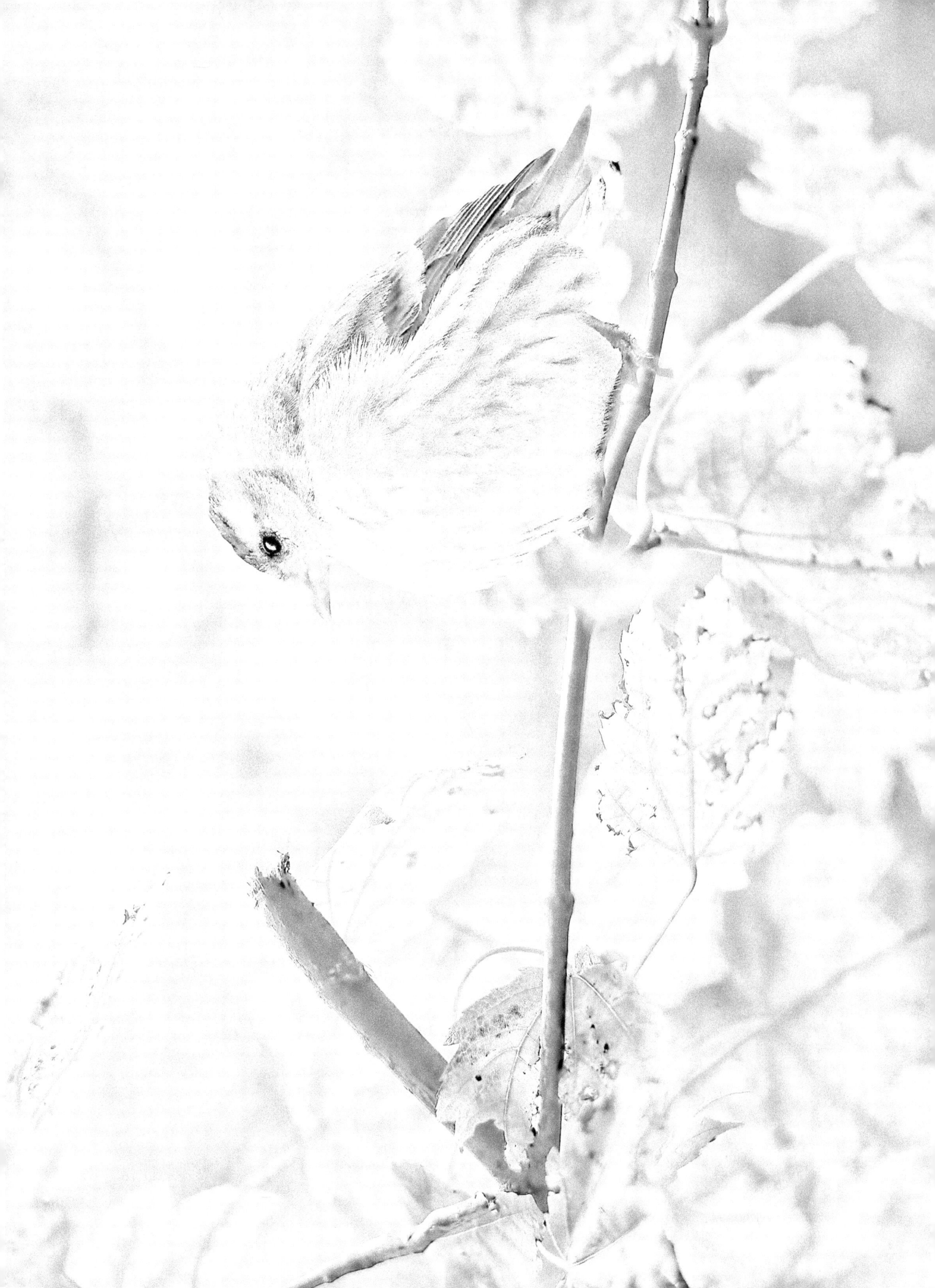

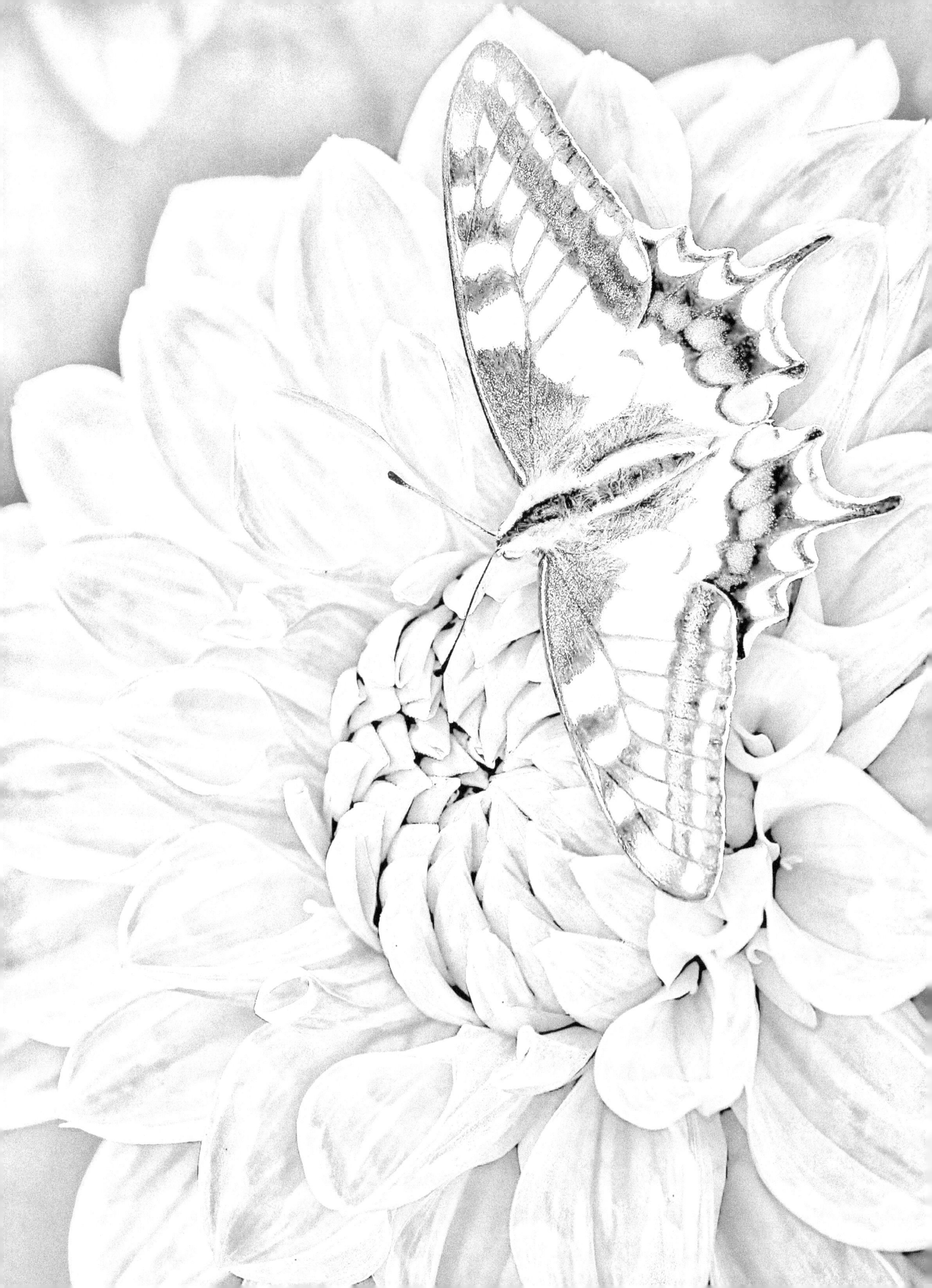

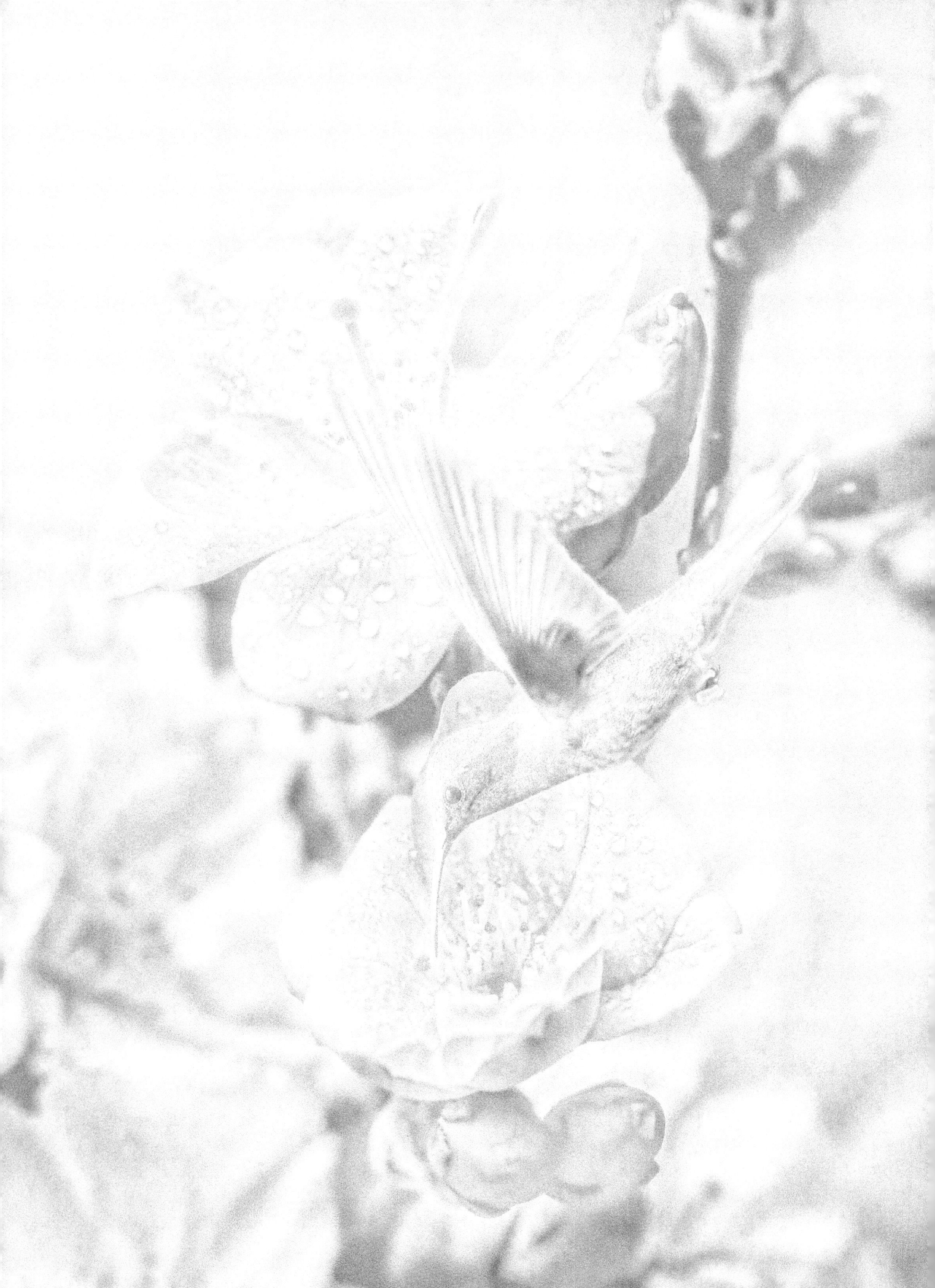

Artwork by l'Œuvre pur

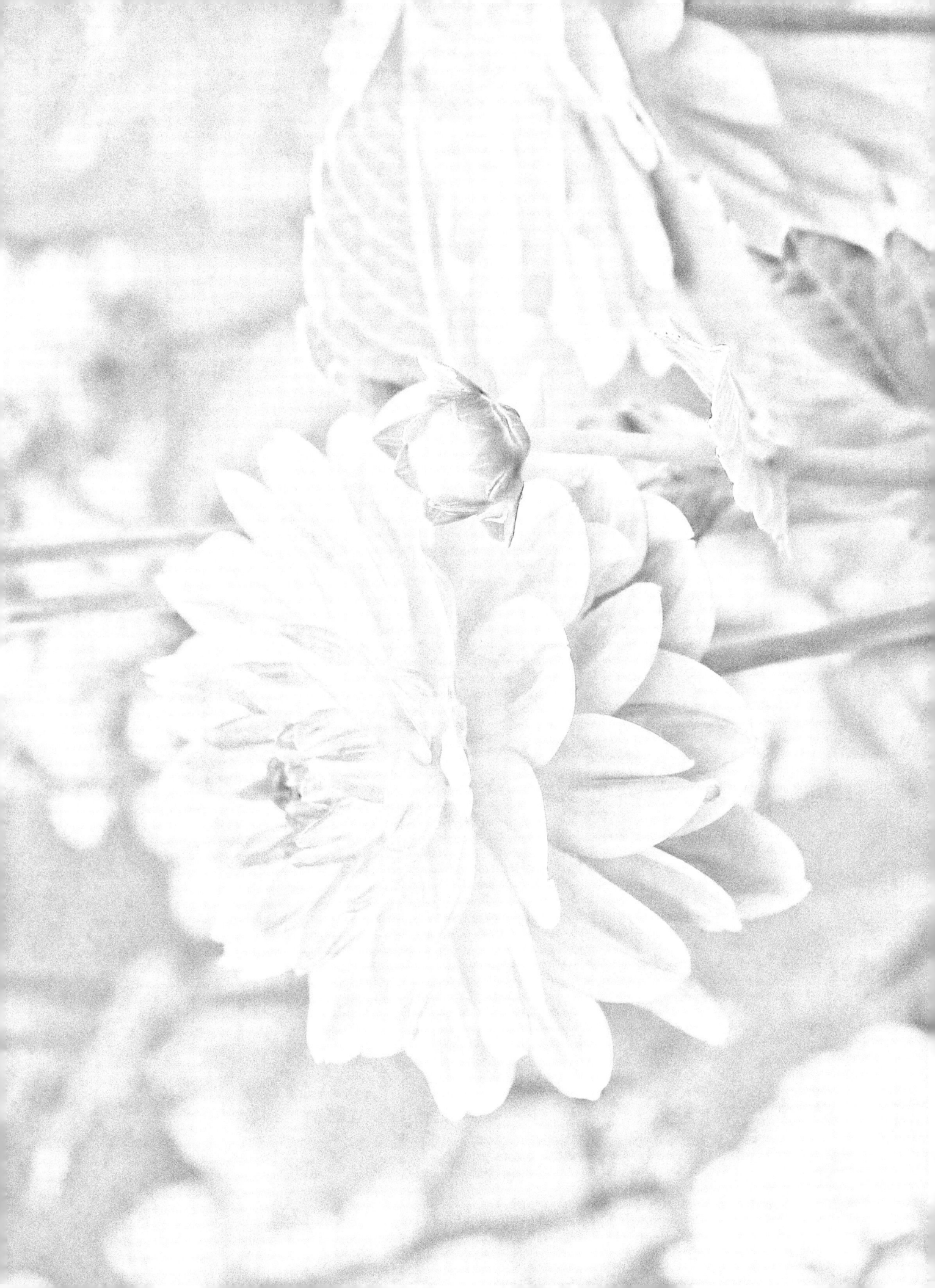

Artwork by / Œuvre par

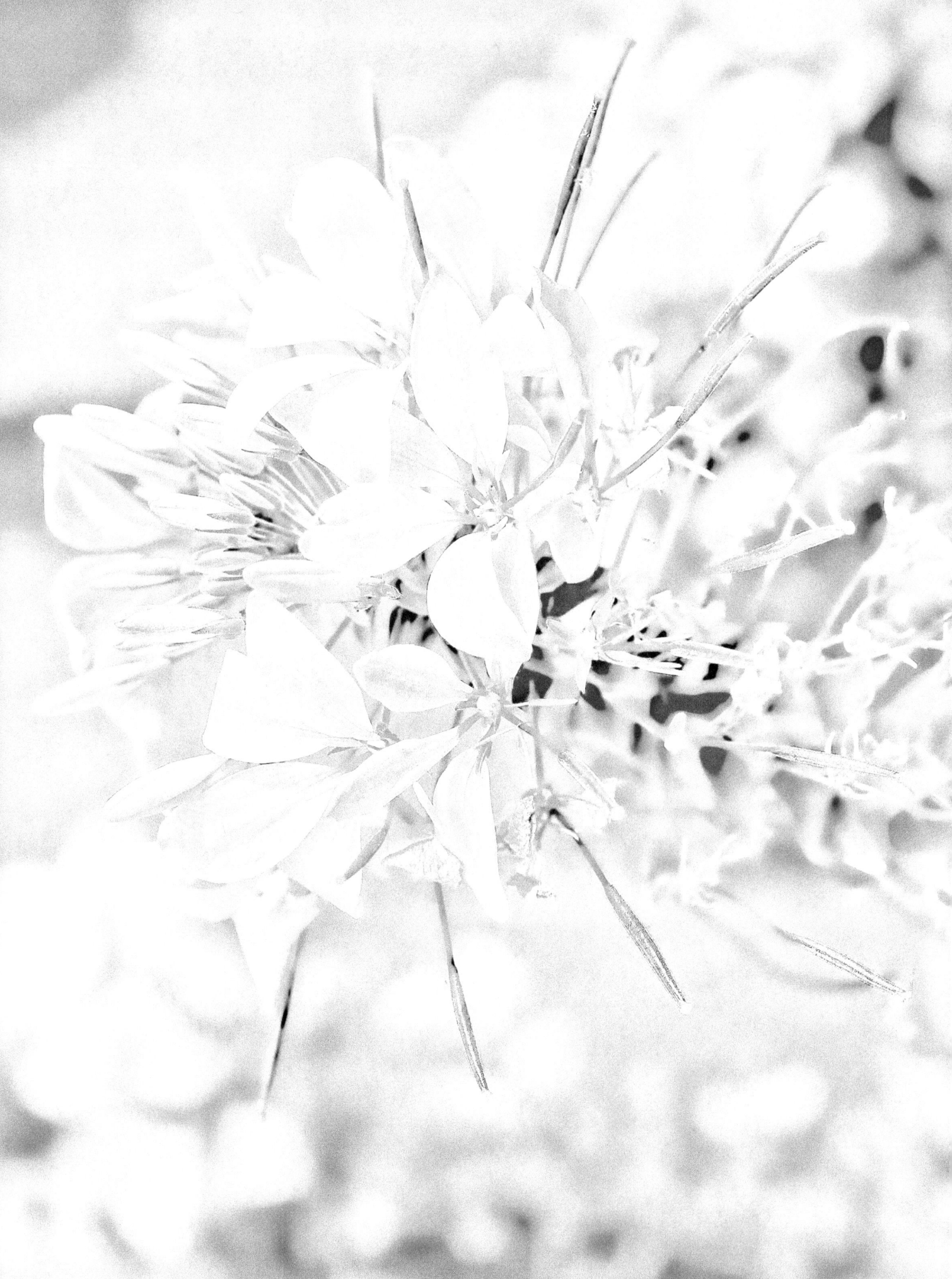

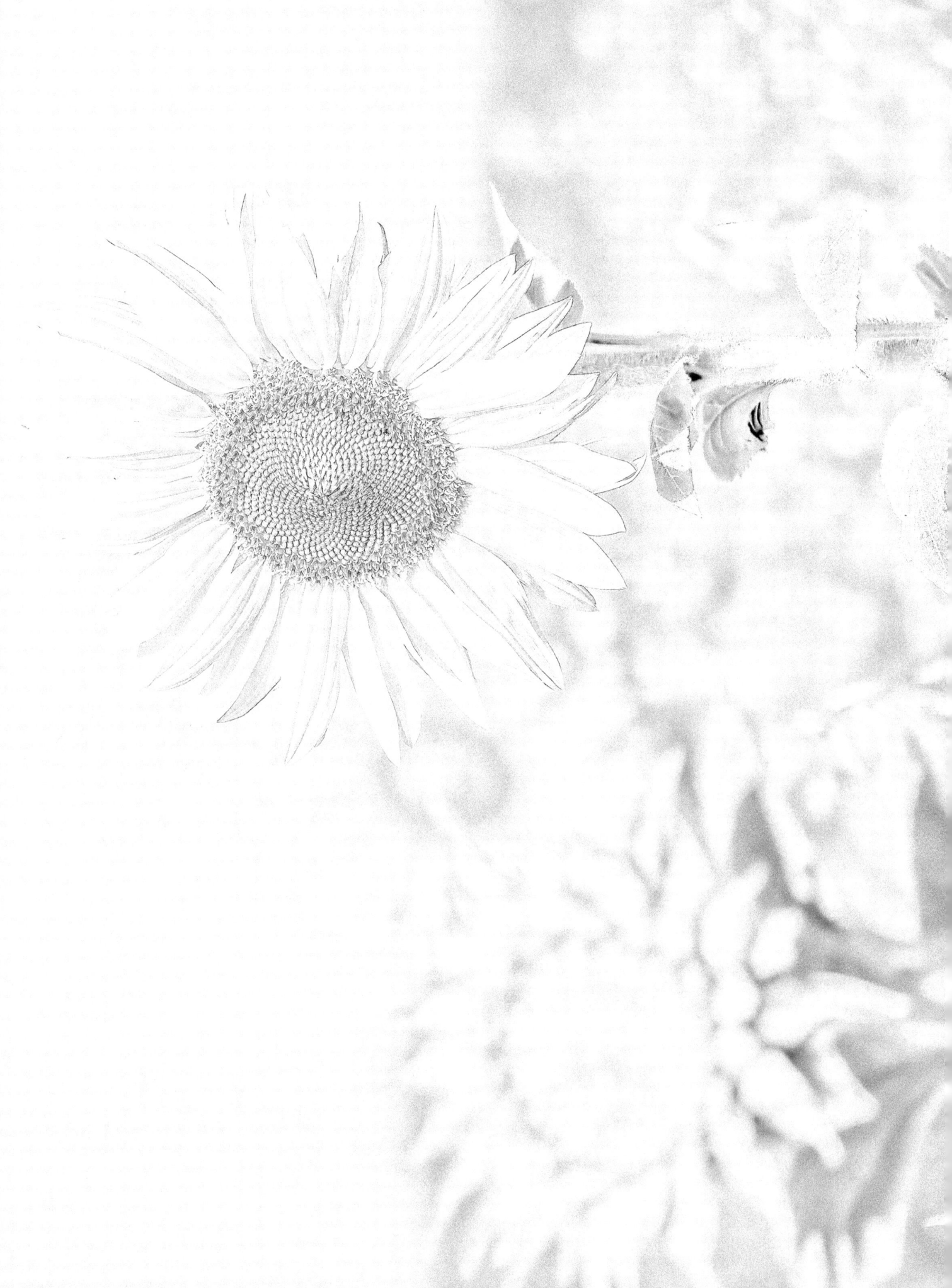

Artwork by l'Œuvre pure

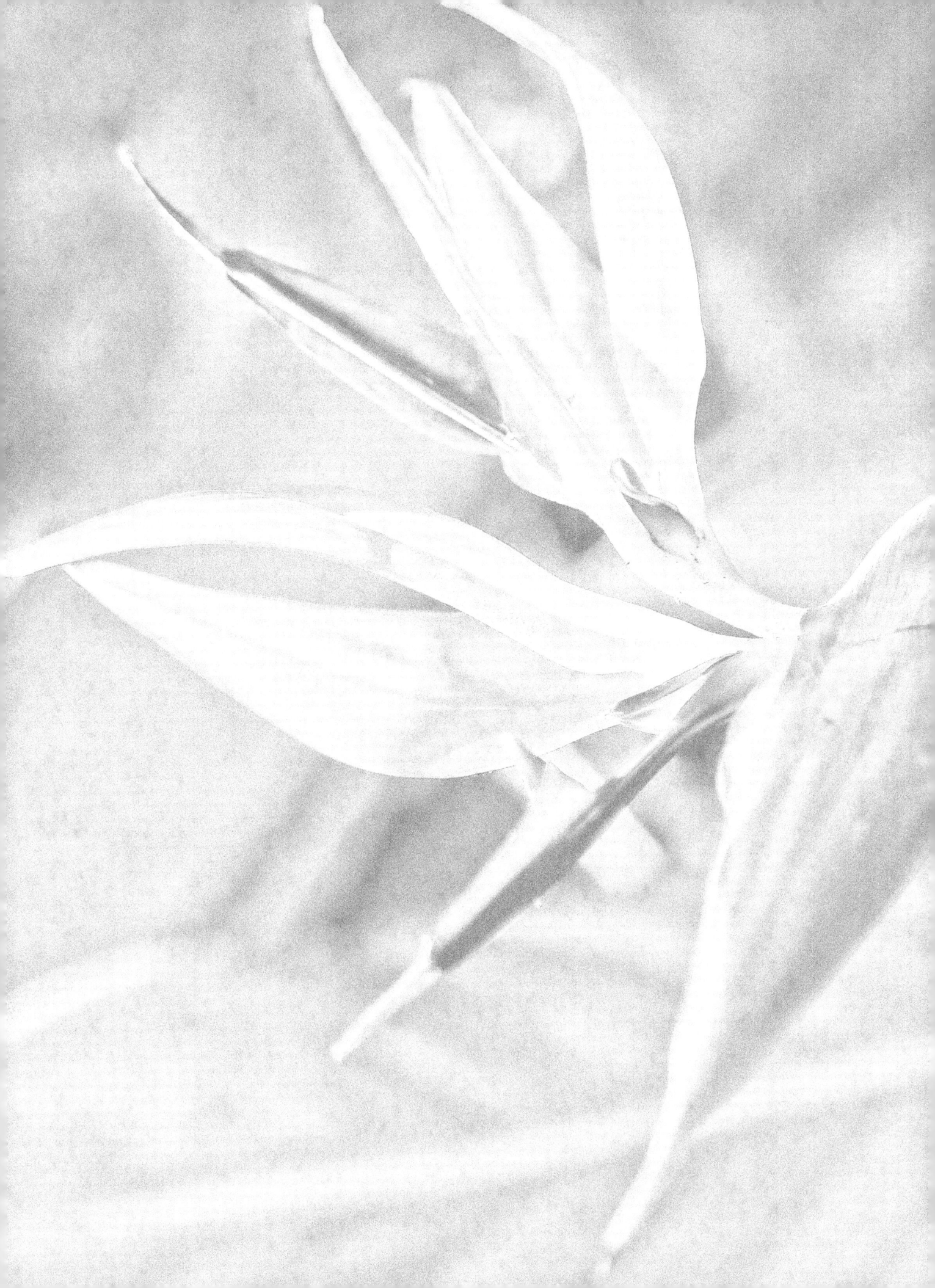

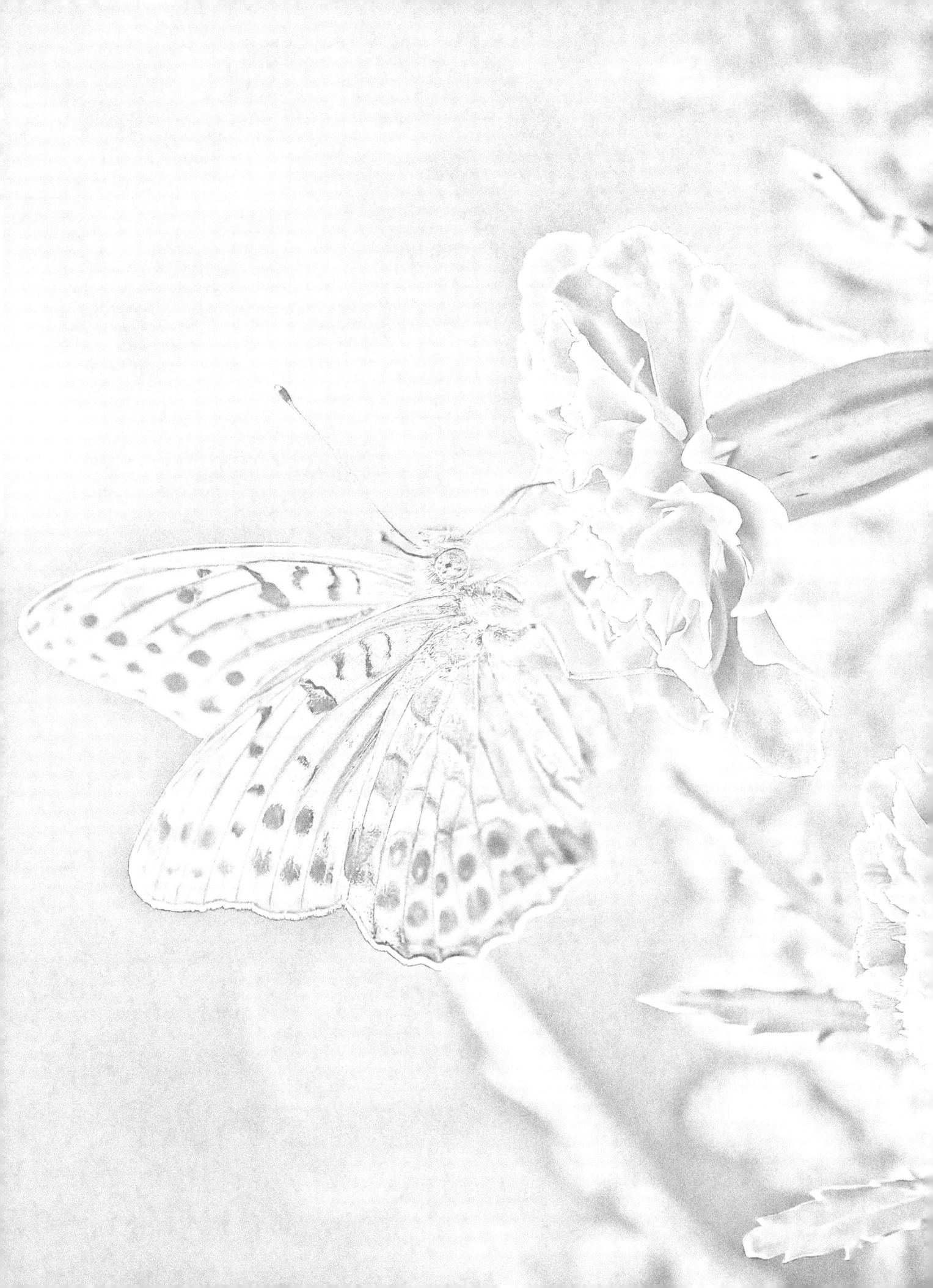

Artwork by l'Œuvre par

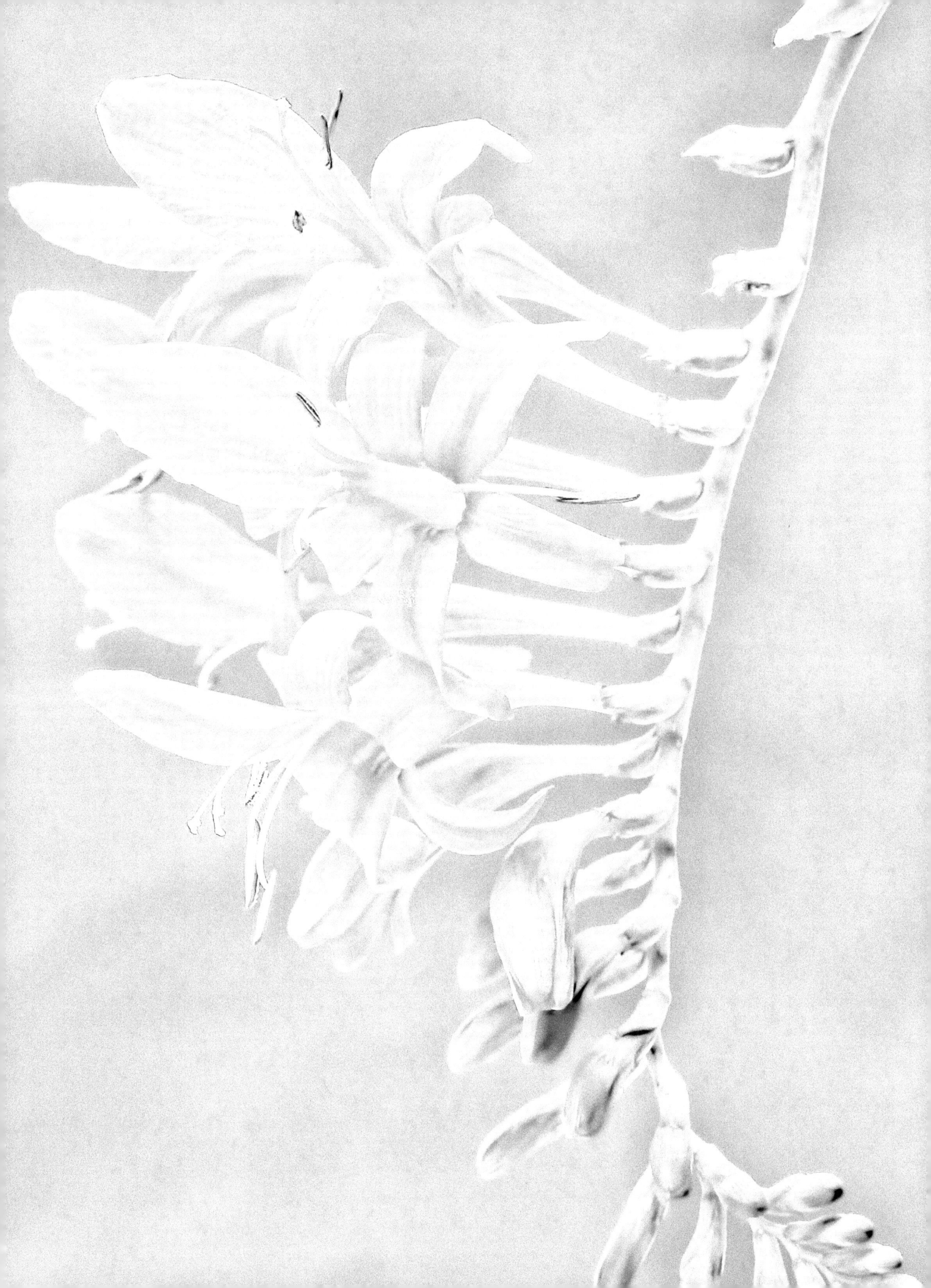

Part 7 – Various Pictures (Low Contrast)

I mean more advanced artists who are not content with coloring childish lines of easy shapes.

When I say "Low Contrast" or "Advanced" I mean different images that are bright or even very bright with less detail visible. The level of "lightening" can vary. That's why you will always find something for yourself.

You can use such a picture as a sketch for your own paintings, on which you can paint your own motifs, or paint almost the entire picture from scratch (using opaque paints) leaving only the main motif from my print, and then adding your own shapes, e.g. rainbow, lights and shadows, elves, spirals, circles, flowers, clouds etc.

I also mean that my painting may only be an inspiration for you, and you will paint something completely different on it. Like a real artist.

Paris, La Seine, France

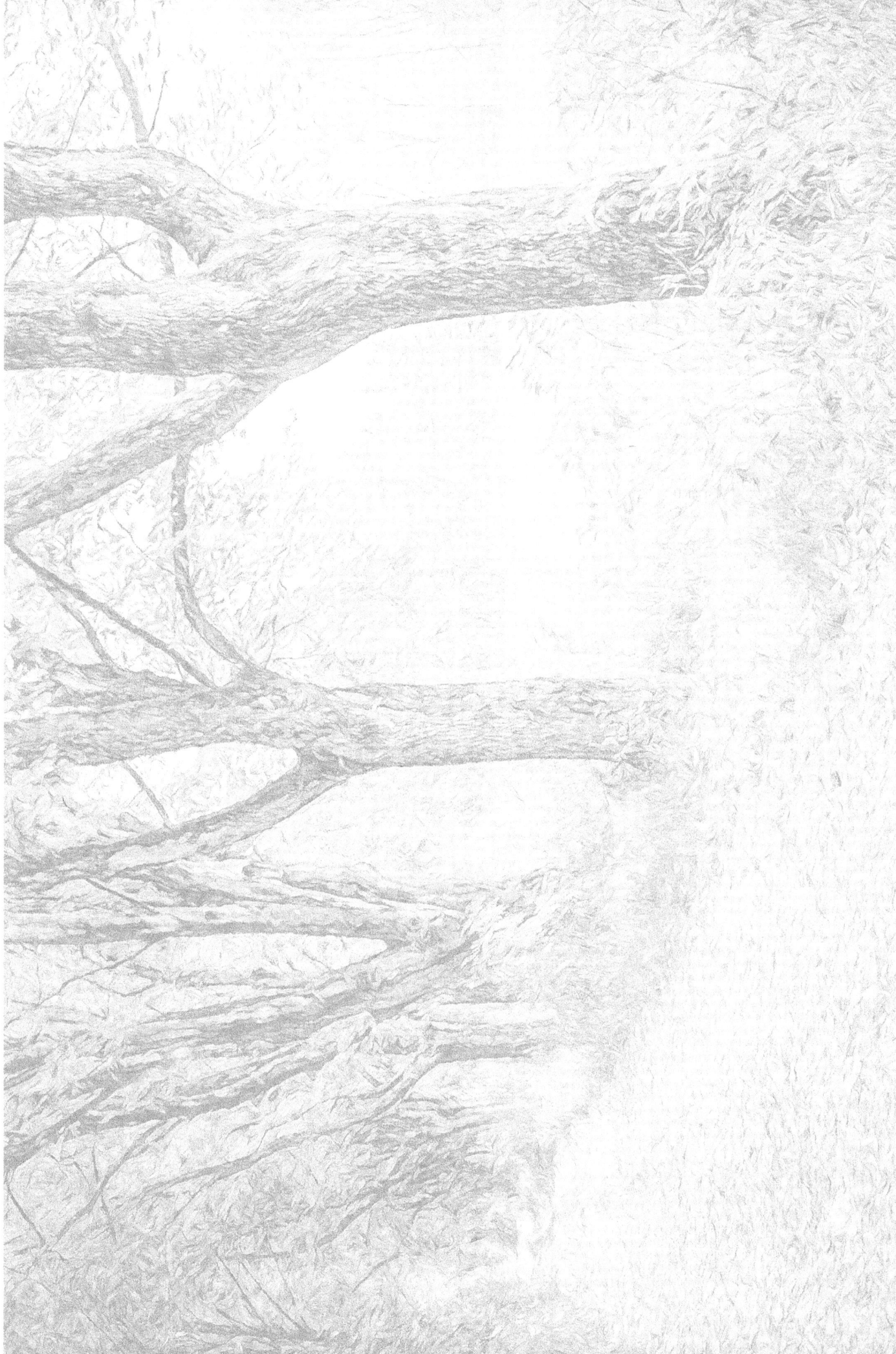

Avenue of trees

Surprise ... out of the box.
My old view painted in 2018.

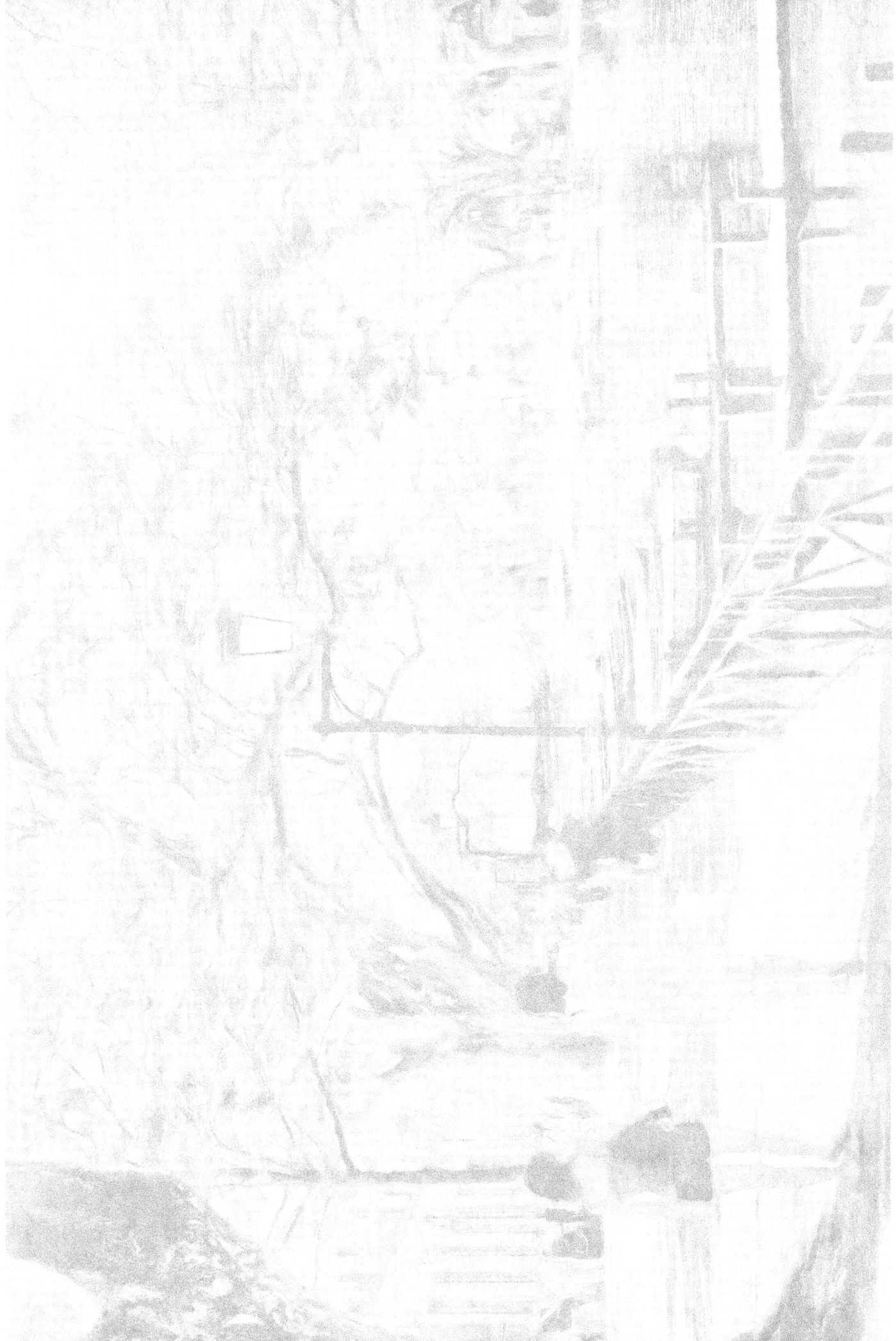

Annecy (France)

Coloring and Painting Guide

1. Optionally: before coloring or painting you can cut all pages out using a long ruler and a craft knife (snap off knife, paper utility knife).

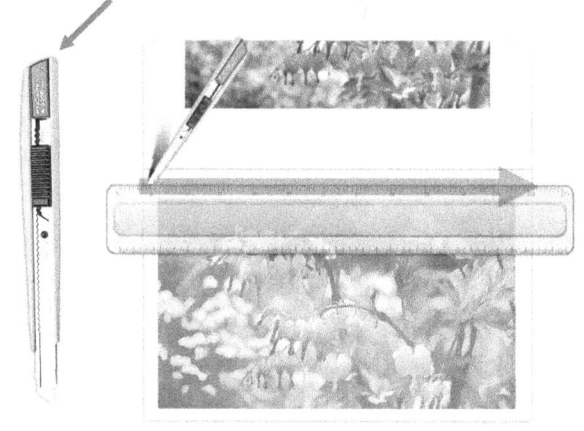
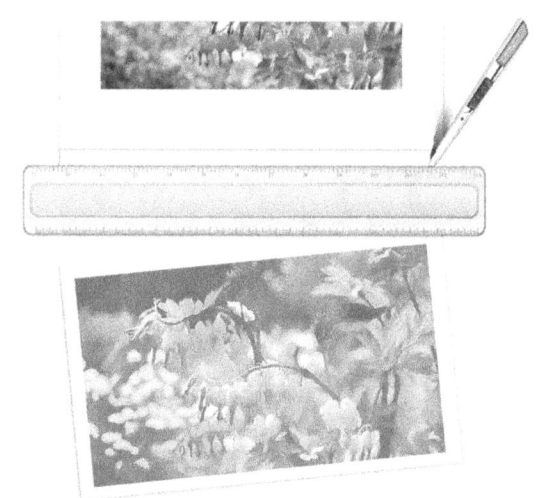

Then place the page on a large sheet of paper or plastic.

2. If the paper curls you can use **paperweights** or **magnets** (in this case you need a metal plate under the picture). Or you can choose a better solution: **"Kenting Magnetic Pad K4M"**

important: a small brush

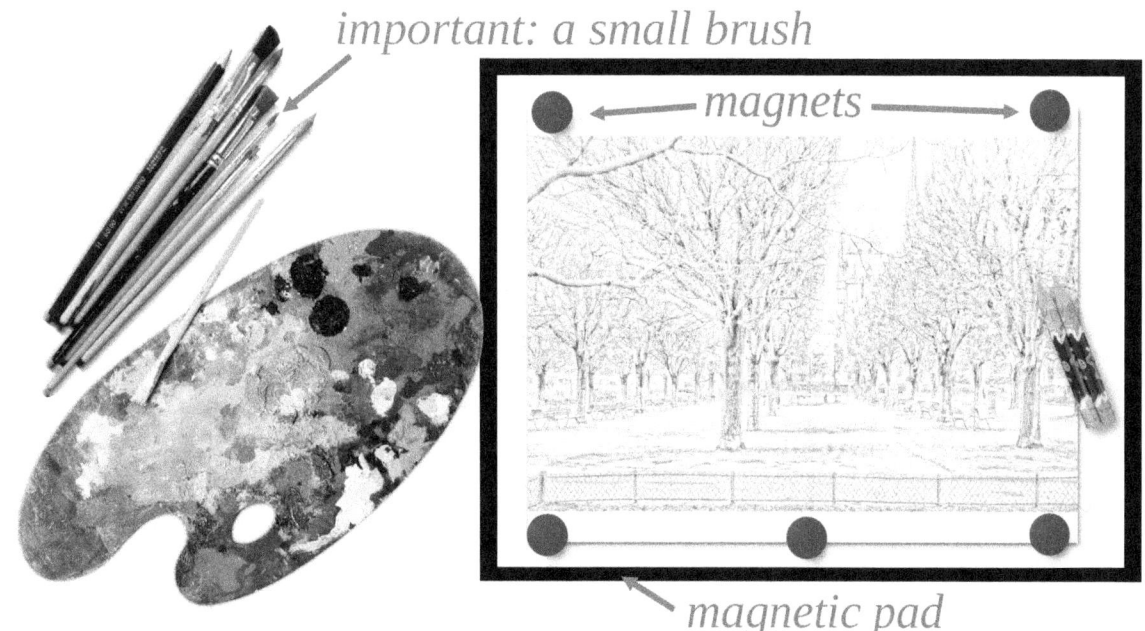

magnets

magnetic pad

About Coloring and Painting

You'll get the best artistic results, painting like, using a **hybrid coloring** method:

1) The first way
- color the fragments with colored pencils
- then use acrylic paints to make the colors more vivid and saturated.

Always allow the paint to dry before applying the next layer.

2) Or the second way
- start with markers
- then finish with Pebbles Chalks (for the background)
A very lovely effect.

About markers. They might bleed through the page, but images are printed on one side. Use a thick cardboard or bristol and put it under your drawing (**if you don't want to cut pages from the book**).

Try also some neon colors and markers. **Pastel pencils** are also a good choice.

Another way: use acrylics only (**acrylics are better than watercolors for this coloring book**), but don't use too much water. This paper doesn't like water. And add some gold and silver paints.

☺ Just try different media and enjoy! Soon you will gain the experience.

Did you know ...

About dark and gray images.

- Every picture can be beautifully colored, even when it is dark or gray (A). How? You can use two methods:

- Apply dark pastel pencils (better) or colored pencils. This will increase the contrast of the image (B).
or
- Cover the gray with bright, opaque acrylic paints (C).

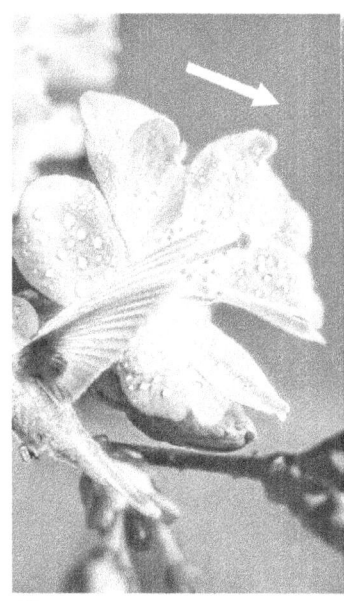

Opaque acrylic paints are best suited for dark images. If you can paint, good work and nice colors will come out because the paint will cover the "ugly", dark print.

- Pastels in the form of pencils also cover well. **Pastel pencils** are better than classic pastels because you can paint small details.

- Acrylic paints give similar effects to oil paints, but are as cheap and easy to use as watercolors. Watercolors are not suitable for this paper and are too transparent, and oil paints require more skills. Meanwhile, acrylic paints combine the advantages of both types, here's the reason why I like them. **There are transparent and opaque acrylic paints**. There are also special gels (e.g: "Gelex") that can brighten colors and make them more opaque.

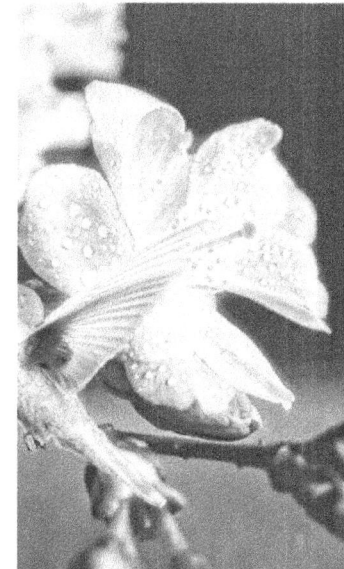

- For these reasons, **do not dilute acrylic paints with water or use less water**. You can mix paints, but rather do not dilute them. If you need a light color, simply mix dark paint with white or yellow.

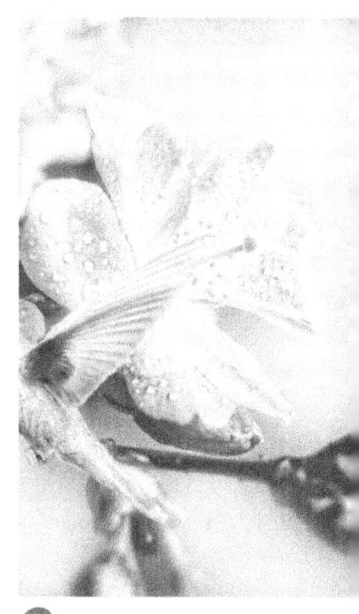

How do you make colors deep, vivid and saturated, just like on the screen?

Colored pencils give a nice effect, but sometimes the picture may be pale, not like my works.

The best effects are created using **hybrid coloring** *and a large number of layers: use black fineliner to draw outlines. Then apply the markers. Next some colored pencils. Also white pencil. Finally, acrylic paints. This method creates beautiful colors and contrast.*

*At this point it is no longer ordinary, amateur coloring, but real art. The effect will be like a painting. See examples on the cover and more on my Amazon page. Soon I will post images on Twitter and YouTube. Soon I will also publish a larger coloring guide and several books in color called "**Coloring Like Painting**".*

People are often surprised that "their coloring" does not give such beautiful effects as on examples.

There are two reasons. The computer screen gives different colors than printing or colored pencils. Secondly, the poor effects result from a lack of experience in using painting techniques and tools.

Search YouTube for grayscale coloring videos. The best colored works look better than the original color photos! And they are simply beautiful and romantic. They have a mood, and the authors paint on them things that were not in the gray photo: flowers, elves, rays of light ...

Don't Give Up!

Some people have habits and favorite tools.

- But if they do not know the differences and nuances, if they do not have knowledge and practice - they get worse results.

For example, Prismacolor is a good brand for drawing, but not for every coloring, because it requires a good paper. Prismacolor Premiers colored pencils is a good choice for bright fragments. But for darker fragments it's better to buy Prismacolor Verithin or Shuttle Art. They have a **harder core** than Premiers, so they better cover the print.

- I also like pastels and other brands that give good results: Coloré, Stabilo and General's. For example:

"Stabilo CarbOthello Pastel Pencil" set - **gives a good pigmentation and performance on thin paper**.

Coloré even produces pencils with metallic colors, including Gold, Green, Blue, Violet, Olive, Lavender, Silver, Indigo, Brown, Black(!). Metallic Black? Why not. See "Coloré Premium Art Pencils Pack".

There are more such things. As I wrote elsewhere, you will gain experience over time and your work will be more and more beautiful. And eventually you will become a master.

At the End

This is my private email, so you can ask me anything you want:
lech.balcerzak.books@gmail.com

Or if you prefer Twitter:
https://twitter.com/LeshekAboutLife

Have a nice day,
Lech

PS
Remember the gold rule: the result does not depend on whether you buy expensive colored pencils and paints. This is a common mistake. The most expensive painting tools from well-known companies will not automatically give you a good effect.

It does not depend on expensive colored pencils or the quality of paper. The effect depends more on your experience. So color, paint and practice. Apply more layers. You will gain practice with time.

www.ingramcontent.com/pod-product-compliance
Lightning Source LLC
Chambersburg PA
CBHW081431220526
45466CB00008B/2347